By Jennifer Appel and Allysa Torey

The Magnolia Bakery Cookbook

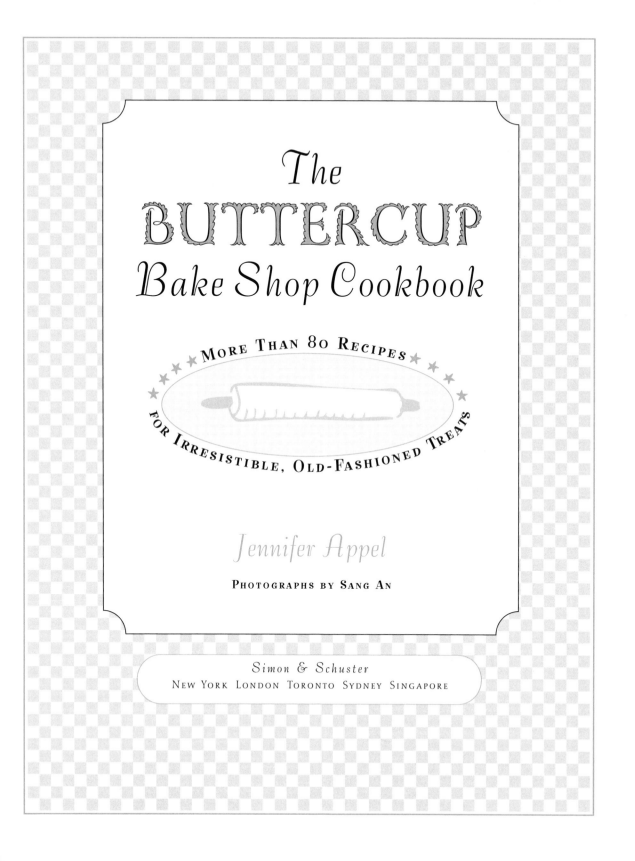

The BUTTERCUP Bake Shop Cookbook

MORE THAN 80 RECIPES

FOR IRRESISTIBLE, OLD-FASHIONED TREATS

Jennifer Appel

PHOTOGRAPHS BY SANG AN

Simon & Schuster
NEW YORK LONDON TORONTO SYDNEY SINGAPORE

SIMON & SCHUSTER
Rockefeller Center
1230 Avenue of the Americas
New York, NY 10020

For information about special discounts for bulk purchases,
please contact Simon & Schuster Special Sales:
1-800-456-6798 or business@simonandschuster.com.

DESIGN AND ILLUSTRATIONS BY JILL WEBER

Manufactured in the United States of America

1 3 5 7 9 10 8 6 4 2

Library of Congress Cataloging-in-Publication Data
Appel, Jennifer.
The Buttercup Bake Shop cookbook : more than 80 recipes for irresistible,
old-fashioned treats / Jennifer Appel ; photographs by Sang An.
p. cm.
1. Baking. 2. Desserts. 3. Buttercup Bake Shop. I. Title.
TX765 .A57 2001
641.8'15–dc21   2001031308
ISBN 0-7432-0579-0

ACKNOWLEDGMENTS

I WOULD ONCE AGAIN LIKE TO THANK MY AGENT, Carla Glasser, for believing another cookbook was in me; my wonderful editor, Sydny Miner, for her support, encouragement, and excitement about more old-fashioned desserts; as well as the Simon & Schuster staff, especially Andrea Mullins and Isolde Sauer.

Also many thanks to photographer Sang An and prop stylist Phillipa Braithwaite.

I am also most grateful to my incredible and tireless staff at Buttercup, who were always enthusiastic "guinea pigs" for my baking creations and offered invaluable feedback. Special thanks must go to Peggy Williams, without whose tremendous help this project would not have been put together in such a short time. Of particular note is her witty and wonderful copy, which "sweetens" the cookbook just so.

And as always, thanks to loving friends and family, and of course, to my customers who keep coming back for more dessert!

Contents

Pies, Crisps, and Cobblers 55

The Breakfast Basket ★ Quick Breads, Biscuits, Coffee Cakes, Buns, and Muffins 69

Seasonal Desserts 83

CONTENTS

Puddings and Custards 95

Fillings and Frostings 105

The
BUTTERCUP
Bake Shop Cookbook

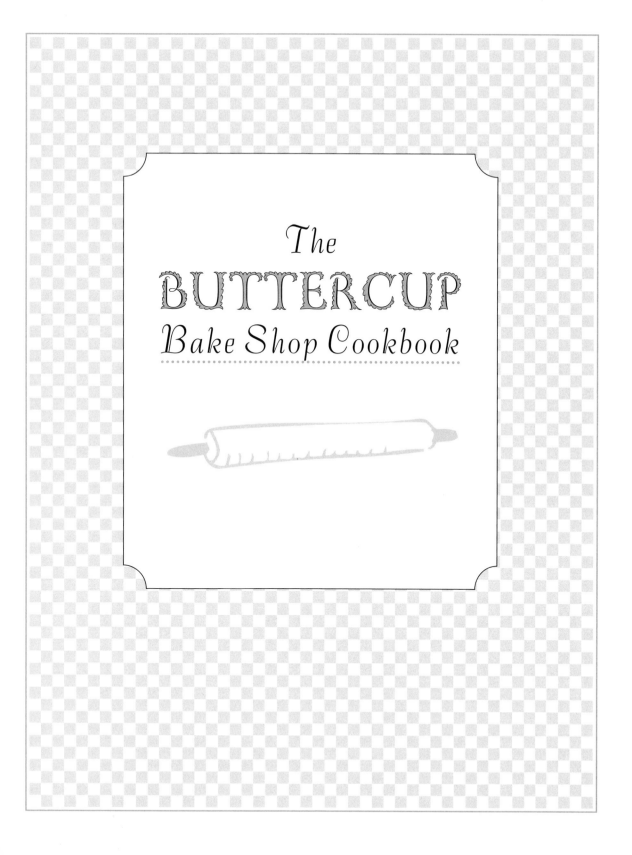

INTRODUCTION

OPENING BUTTERCUP BAKE SHOP HAS BEEN A WONDERFUL NEXT STEP FOR me after founding and running New York's Greenwich Village legend, The Magnolia Bakery. Now I can offer a wider spectrum of goods to customers while also filling the needs of our midtown fans. More ovens and more space has provided greater occasion to be creative and produce a bigger array of old-fashioned treats.

Buttercup Bake Shop is a place to walk into and feel deliciously overwhelmed by display cases filled with cupcakes every color of the rainbow, counters crowded with classic American layer cakes, and "just like Grandma's" muffins, buns, cookies, bars, squares, and more. Customers tell me they feel embraced by childhood memories of their neighborhood bake shop. These classic desserts are satisfying the midtown neighborhood folk as well as the most prestigious of clients; Bloomingdale's, Saks Fifth Avenue, Bergdorf Goodman, Tiffany's, *New York* magazine, *Entertainment Weekly*, Miramax Films, DreamWorks, the David Letterman show, and many Broadway theaters, among others, have all been celebrating their special occasions with these delightfully delicious cakes and cupcakes.

My first cookbook, *The Magnolia Bakery Cookbook*, coauthored with Allysa Torey, has succeeded in helping bakers, both novice and seasoned, in creating luscious homemade desserts. *The Buttercup Bake Shop Cookbook*, a natural follow-up, includes more than eighty recipes that will entice you further and will be a passport into the world of old-fashioned baking.

As we edge into the new millennium, the comfort of time-warp baking maintains its appeal. With information moving at the speed of light, Buttercup Bake Shop lets you slow down, hear your favorite old jazz tunes, and while away an afternoon sipping your favorite beverage and enjoying some delectable, nostalgic treats. Return to your fantasy of childhood and bake these satisfying desserts that spell comfort and love.

HELPFUL HINTS

BAKING, LIKE EVERYTHING ELSE, HAS ITS BASIC RULES. THE RULES ARE NOT complex, but learn and follow them in order to create a dessert you can be proud of. These suggestions will refer mostly to layer cakes, pies, muffins, and cake icings, which are usually the more difficult aspects of baking for the novice.

I find that using the right ingredients is crucial to home baking, on a small or large scale. I use only whole milk for my recipes, and sugar is granulated unless otherwise specified. When using confectioners' (powdered) sugar, make sure to sift out any lumps before using, or it may result in an uneven texture in your cake or frosting.

Extracts are always pure, because imitation tends to impart a less-rich flavor; the same goes for the use of juices and zests.

Use the best-quality dairy ingredients, and bake with imported chocolate when possible (use only the best-quality domestic chocolate if you cannot find imported). Cocoa powder is always used unsweetened in this book, and can be Dutch-processed, but this is not necessary.

All-purpose flour can be bleached or unbleached, but my preference is unbleached. Flour does not always need to be sifted, but sifting is strongly suggested in certain recipes as it creates a certain lightness of texture necessary to many desserts. Make sure to use the type of flour specified, as in cake flour or self-rising flour, or your recipe will not work as expected.

I find that large eggs are the best for baking and produce the most consistent results.

Before starting any recipe, always read through the recipe from beginning to end to make sure that you thoroughly understand it. Then, assemble your ingredients and equipment before beginning, in order to make the process flow more smoothly.

Take out butter, cream cheese, and eggs from the refrigerator at least 1 hour before starting the recipe. The butter will be easier to cream, and the eggs will beat up better.

Layer Cakes

When using metal pans, for layer cakes especially, make sure they are smooth and clean, because uneven or blackened pans tend to absorb heat unevenly. Grease the pans by using a pastry brush, or by rubbing on butter or shortening with your fingers or a paper towel. After greasing, sprinkle a few spoonfuls of flour into the pan and shake it around until the entire inside of the pan is coated with flour. Empty out the excess flour by gently tapping the pan. Line the bottom of the pan with waxed paper or parchment. This will help prevent the cake from sticking to the pan.

When creaming butter, it is important to beat the butter until it is light and fluffy. I strongly recommend the use of a good handheld or standing mixer for this, but it can be done by hand as well. Gradually add the sugar, beating all the while, and continue to beat for 2 or 3 minutes. Add the eggs one at a time, beating vigorously, until the mixture is thick, fluffy, and pale in color.

To make it easier to add the ingredients in an alternating fashion, thoroughly combine the dry ingredients in a bowl or large measuring cup, and mix the liquids together with any extracts in a separate measuring cup. When adding the wet and dry ingredients, do so alternately, usually in two or three parts, beating after each addition until the ingredients are blended thoroughly and the batter is smooth. However, do not overbeat or the cake can turn out to be dry or tough. Use a rubber spatula to scrape down the sides of the bowl, making sure the ingredients are well blended and are not "hiding" near the bottom.

When using egg whites in a recipe, beat them until relatively stiff but not dry. Overbeating the whites can produce a dry cake. Mix in the whites a third at a time, "easing" them into the batter. Place the beaten whites into the center of the bowl and, using a rubber spatula, gently fold them using a light up-and-over motion. Make sure not to stir or beat, or you will lose the air in the whites.

When pouring cake batter into pans, spread it evenly with a spatula so that the batter is level. You can use a measuring cup if needed to make sure an equal amount of batter is in each pan.

Pies

While many feel baking pies can be a bit daunting, a little practice is all it takes to get the feel of what the pie dough is supposed to be like. It also takes a little time to develop a light hand so that you can work the dough without *over*working it.

If you've never rolled out your own piecrust, it might be a good idea to start with one that calls for shortening instead of butter. Shortening is used at room temperature, which tends to make it easier to work with. Feel free to substitute shortening in my recipes; however, butter crusts are worth getting used to because of their very flaky and moist texture. Remember to handle your dough as little as possible, because overworking pie dough tends to toughen it. Start out with the dry ingredients in a bowl, then add in the butter (or shortening) cut into bits. Work quickly with a pastry blender and mix the ingredients together until they resemble coarse crumbs. When adding the water, make sure it is very cold (preferably ice water). Sprinkle the water lightly, but do not pour it in, because this can produce an uneven dough, meaning some parts are too dry and some parts are too wet. If the dough is too dry, sprinkle a little more water over it. Then, with your hands, knead the dough together several times, just enough to form it into a ball.

Using two sheets of waxed paper can be helpful when rolling out a piecrust. Place the dough in the center of one sheet of paper (about 12 x 12 inches) and place the remaining sheet over that. With a rolling pin, roll out the dough to about a ⅛-inch thickness, using short, quick movements. Transfer the dough to a cookie sheet, still between the waxed sheets, and refrigerate for about 20 minutes or so. Peel off the top layer of waxed paper and invert the dough into a pie plate. Press it lightly into the bottom of the plate first, then up the sides. Press the overhang of the crust downward around the edges, and cut off any remaining dough with a sharp knife. Press the outer edges of the crust into the rim of the plate. Use the tines of a fork to make a pattern, or using your fingers, crimp the edges to make a fluted design.

Muffins

An important thing to remember when baking muffins is to *gently* mix the batter until the dry ingredients are just moistened by the wet ingredients. Overmixing, or using too strong a hand, will result in deflated, dense muffins. Quick breads are made with a similar technique, although they are a bit heartier and less likely to become dense. Buns (the nonyeast variety) usually are made with a technique similar to cakes, in that the butter and sugar are creamed, and therefore are likely to rise easily—they are more foolproof than muffins.

Cake Icings

Before icing a layer cake, be sure the cake is absolutely cold. Icing will not stick to a warm cake, and a warm cake can become soggy if iced too soon.

Brush all the crumbs off the sides of the cake layers and place the layers top side up (pan side down) on a level surface. Do not frost the bottom of the cake, which was in contact with the pan.

Layer cakes should be frosted (or spread with filling) between the layers first. Put the layers together, taking care that the edges are even and the cake is the same height all over. Next frost the top, and then the sides of the cake. Use a generous amount of icing and make sure to cover all the surface area of your cake.

Cakes ★ Layer Cakes and Other Classics

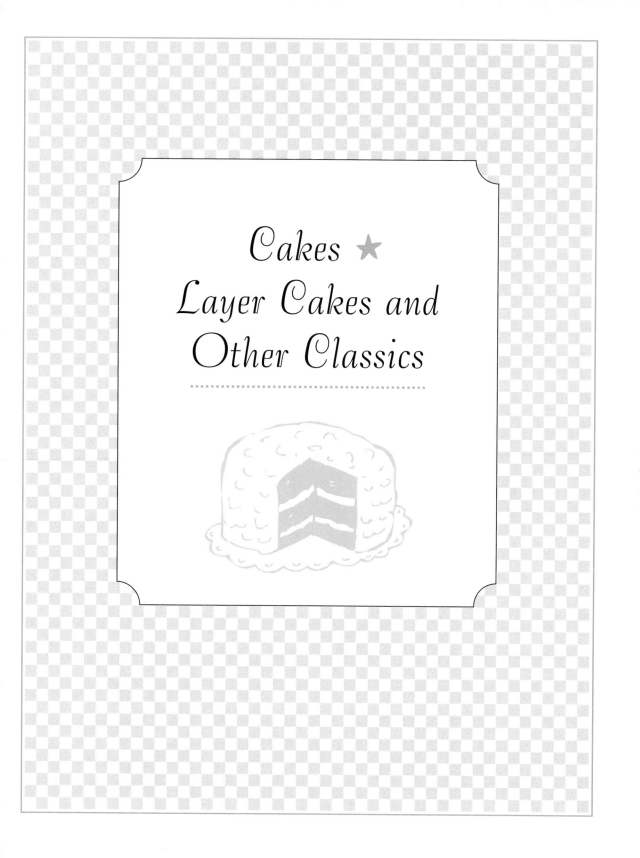

Angel Food Cake

> *While I count myself among the many afraid of making angel food cake (all those egg whites!), I discovered that following the directions carefully assures producing a perfect cake, even the first time around. It's best to use a standing mixer for this recipe, but you can use a handheld mixer if necessary.*

Preheat oven to 375 degrees. Set out an ungreased 10-inch tube pan.

In a medium bowl, combine the flour with one cup of the sugar. Sift these together three separate times. Set this aside and place remaining sugar in a separate cup for later use.

Place the egg whites in a standing mixer bowl and, using the whisk attachment, turn mixer to lowest speed. After 1 minute, add the cream of tartar, vanilla, and salt. After another minute of beating, turn the mixer to medium speed and gradually add the reserved ½ cup sugar.

Stop and scrape the sides of the bowl with a rubber spatula when all the sugar has been added. Resume beating until whites are stiff but moist. This should take about 3 to 5 minutes.

Transfer the egg whites to a large bowl. Sift the flour-sugar mixture over the whites and gently fold until all the dry ingredients are mixed in.

Fill the pan immediately and smooth top with rubber spatula. Bake for 30 to 40 minutes. Test for doneness at 30 minutes. If tester comes out clean with no traces of batter, it is done. The cake should be lightly browned and spring back when pressed gently with a finger. Remove from oven and allow to cool in pan for 30 minutes. Place the pan upside down on an empty bottle for easier removal. Remove the cake from pan and cool completely on a wire rack.

MAKES ONE 10-INCH CAKE; SERVES 10 TO 12.

1 cup cake flour

1½ cups sugar

13 or 14 large egg whites (2 cups)

1½ teaspoons cream of tartar

1 teaspoon vanilla extract

¼ teaspoon salt

Apple Pecan Cake

A nice, dense cake, perfect for an afternoon tea.

CAKE

3 cups all-purpose flour

2 cups sugar

½ teaspoon baking soda

½ teaspoon salt

1 cup plus 2 tablespoons
   vegetable oil

3 large eggs, at room
   temperature

1 teaspoon vanilla extract

2 Golden Delicious apples,
   peeled, cut into 1-inch
   pieces (about 2 cups)

1 cup coarsely chopped
   pecans, plus ¼ cup for
   garnish

GLAZE

1½ cups confectioners' sugar

2 tablespoons water (more if
   needed)

Preheat oven to 350 degrees.

Lightly grease a 10-inch tube pan.

To make the cake: Sift together the flour, sugar, baking soda, and salt into a large mixing bowl, making a well in the center. Stir in the oil, eggs, and vanilla. Stir in the apples and pecans.

Spoon the batter into the prepared pan. Bake for 60 to 70 minutes, or until a cake tester inserted into the center of the cake comes out clean. Let cake cool in pan for 20 minutes. Remove from pan and cool completely on a wire rack.

To make the glaze: Stir together the sugar and water in a small bowl until smooth. Drizzle decoratively over cooled cake. Garnish with pecans if desired.

MAKES ONE 10-INCH CAKE; SERVES 10 TO 12.

Applesauce Layer Cake

Here's my version of this legendary American classic. Raisins and nuts can be optional, but they lend a nice touch to this astoundingly moist cake. Ice this with Cream Cheese Icing (page 112).

Preheat oven to 350 degrees.

Grease and lightly flour two 9 x 2-inch round cake pans. Line the bottoms with waxed paper.

In a medium bowl, sift together the flour, baking soda, salt, cinnamon, and ginger. Set aside.

In a large bowl, on the medium speed of an electric mixer, cream the butter and sugar until smooth, about 3 minutes. Beat in the egg until thoroughly blended, then beat in the applesauce. Add the dry ingredients in thirds, alternating with the buttermilk, beating after each addition until smooth. Mix in the nuts and raisins.

Divide the batter between the prepared pans. Bake for 35 to 45 minutes or until a cake tester inserted into the center of the cake comes out clean. Let cake cool in pans for 10 minutes. Remove from pans and cool completely on a wire rack.

When cake has cooled, ice between the layers, then ice top and sides of cake.

MAKES 1 TWO-LAYER 9-INCH CAKE; SERVES 10 TO 12.

3 cups cake flour

1½ teaspoons baking soda

1½ teaspoons salt

¾ teaspoon cinnamon

½ teaspoon ground ginger

½ cup (1 stick) unsalted butter, softened

2 cups sugar

1 large egg, at room temperature

1½ cups unsweetened applesauce

1 cup buttermilk

½ cup chopped walnuts

1 cup golden raisins

Aunt Sadie's Fabulous Pound Cake

> Well, I didn't have an Aunt Sadie, but somebody did! Here's a twist on a perfectly wonderful pound cake, found in a vintage cookbook, that both refrigerates and freezes well.

2 cups cake flour

1 teaspoon baking powder

2 teaspoons unsweetened cocoa powder

¼ teaspoon salt

½ teaspoon cinnamon

½ teaspoon nutmeg

1 cup (2 sticks) unsalted butter, softened

1 cup sugar

¼ cup milk

1 tablespoon brandy

½ teaspoon vanilla extract

4 large egg whites

Preheat oven to 350 degrees.

Grease and lightly flour a 9 x 5 x 3-inch loaf pan.

In a medium bowl, sift together the flour, baking powder, cocoa, salt, cinnamon, and nutmeg. Set aside.

In a large bowl, on the medium speed of an electric mixer, cream the butter and the sugar until fluffy, about 3 minutes. Add the dry ingredients in two parts, alternating with the milk, beating well after each addition. Add the brandy and vanilla.

In a separate bowl, on the high speed of an electric mixer, beat the egg whites until soft peaks form. Gently fold into batter, making sure no streaks of white are showing.

Pour the batter into the prepared pan. Bake 45 to 55 minutes or until a cake tester inserted into the center of the cake comes out clean. Let cake cool in pan for 20 minutes. Remove from pan and cool completely on a wire rack.

MAKES 1 LOAF CAKE; SERVES 8 TO 10.

Buttercup Golden Layer Cake

The quintessential birthday cake—definitely our most popular birthday seller, topped with Classic American Buttercream (page 110) or Classic Chocolate Buttercream (page 111).

1 cup (2 sticks) unsalted butter, softened

2 cups sugar

4 large eggs, at room temperature

1 cup milk

1 teaspoon vanilla extract

1½ cups self-rising flour

1¼ cups all-purpose flour

Preheat oven to 350 degrees.

Grease and lightly flour three 9 x 2-inch round cake pans. Line the bottoms with waxed paper.

In a large bowl, on the medium speed of an electric mixer, cream the butter and sugar until fluffy, about 3 minutes. Add the eggs, one at a time, beating well after each addition. Mix the milk and vanilla together. Combine the flours and add in two parts, alternating with the milk and vanilla mixture, beating well after each addition.

Divide the batter among the prepared pans. Bake for 20 to 25 minutes or until a cake tester inserted into the center of the cake comes out clean. Let cake cool in pans for 10 minutes. Remove from pans and cool completely on wire rack.

If you're making cupcakes, line two 12-cup muffin tins with cupcake papers. Spoon the batter into the cups about three-quarters full. Bake until the tops spring back when lightly touched, about 20 to 22 minutes. Remove cupcakes from pans and cool completely on a rack before icing.

When cake has cooled, ice between the layers, then ice top and sides of cake.

MAKES 1 THREE-LAYER 9-INCH CAKE OR 24 CUPCAKES;
SERVES 10 TO 12.

Caramel Cake with Brown Sugar Frosting

A very popular choice among my cookbook tasters—a cake with a unique flavor and stupendous icing, especially winning with the caramel-loving crowd.

CAKE

2½ cups all-purpose flour

2½ teaspoons baking powder

1 teaspoon salt

½ cup (1 stick) unsalted butter, softened

1⅓ cups sugar

3 large eggs, at room temperature

1 cup Caramel (page 108) plus ½ cup water, combined

FROSTING

2 cups firmly packed light brown sugar

½ cup heavy cream

6 tablespoons (¾ stick) unsalted butter, softened

2½ cups sifted confectioners' sugar

Preheat oven to 350 degrees.

Grease and lightly flour two 9 x 2-inch round cake pans. Line the bottoms with waxed paper.

To make the cake: In a medium bowl, sift together the flour, baking powder, and salt. Set aside.

In a large bowl, on the medium speed of an electric mixer, cream the butter and sugar until fluffy, about 3 minutes. Add the eggs, one at a time, beating well after each addition. Add the dry ingredients in thirds, alternating with the caramel mixture, beating after each addition until smooth.

Divide the batter between the prepared pans and bake for 30 to 35 minutes, or until a cake tester inserted into the center of the cake comes out clean. Let cake cool in pans for 10 minutes. Remove from pans and cool completely on a wire rack.

To make the frosting: In a heavy-bottomed saucepan, place the brown sugar, cream, and butter. Cook over medium heat, stirring constantly, until mixture comes to a boil. Boil for 5 minutes without stirring. Remove from heat and let cool for about 20 to 30 minutes. Add the confectioners' sugar and beat with an electric mixer until the frosting is perfectly smooth. If too thick, beat in a bit more heavy cream.

When cake has cooled, ice between the layers, then ice top and sides of cake.

MAKES 1 TWO-LAYER 9-INCH CAKE; SERVES 10 TO 12.

Carrot Cake

Just about the best carrot cake you've ever tasted; it is the number-one seller at Buttercup, hands down. Ice this with Cream Cheese Icing (page 112), or bake this recipe in two loaf pans and enjoy it as a moist and tasty quick bread.

Preheat oven to 350 degrees.

Grease and lightly flour three 9 x 2-inch round cake pans, or two 9 x 5 x 3-inch loaf pans. Line the bottoms with waxed paper.

In a medium bowl, whisk together the flour, baking powder, baking soda, cinnamon, allspice, and ginger. Set aside.

In a large bowl, on the medium speed of an electric mixer, cream the butter and sugars until fluffy, about 3 minutes. Beat in the eggs, one at a time. Beat in the vanilla. Add the dry ingredients in thirds to the butter mixture, alternating with the apple juice. Beat for 45 seconds after each addition, beginning and ending with the flour mixture. Stir in the carrots, apple, pecans, and cream until all the ingredients are well incorporated.

Divide the batter among the prepared pans and bake for 30 to 35 minutes or until a cake tester inserted into the center of the cake comes out clean. Let cake cool in pans for 10 minutes. Remove from pans and cool completely on a wire rack (see Note).

When cake has cooled, ice between the layers, and then on top. It is not necessary to ice the entire cake, but you may do so.

MAKES 1 THREE-LAYER, 9-INCH CAKE OR TWO LOAVES; SERVES 10 TO 12.

★ NOTE: THESE LAYERS ARE VERY DELICATE, SO USE CARE WHEN REMOVING FROM PANS.

2½ cups all-purpose flour

1 teaspoon baking powder

1 teaspoon baking soda

1 teaspoon cinnamon

½ teaspoon allspice

½ teaspoon ground ginger

1½ cups (3 sticks) unsalted butter, softened

1 cup firmly packed light brown sugar

1 cup sugar

3 large eggs, at room temperature

2 teaspoons vanilla extract

½ cup apple juice (any brand)

1½ cups peeled, grated carrots (about 3 to 4 medium carrots)

1 Golden Delicious apple, peeled and diced (about 1 cup)

1 cup finely chopped pecans

3 tablespoons heavy cream

Fireside Orange Cake with Brandy Glaze

An old family favorite that got its name from the cold wintry night we huddled around the fireplace with this delicious and tangy cake.

2 cups all-purpose flour

1 teaspoon baking soda

¼ teaspoon salt

½ cup (1 stick) unsalted butter, softened

1 cup firmly packed light brown sugar

2 large eggs, at room temperature

¼ teaspoon lemon extract

½ teaspoon vanilla extract

1 cup milk

1 large orange

¼ cup blanched almonds

½ cup golden raisins

½ cup chopped dates

⅓ cup sugar

3 tablespoons brandy

Preheat oven to 350 degrees. Grease and lightly flour a 9 x 2-inch springform pan.

In a medium bowl, sift together the flour, baking soda, and salt. Set aside.

In a large bowl, on the medium speed of an electric mixer, cream the butter and brown sugar until fluffy, about 3 minutes. Add the eggs one at a time. Add the lemon and vanilla extracts to the milk and stir into batter, alternating with the flour mixture. Halve the orange and squeeze, reserving about ½ cup of juice. In a food processor, grind orange rind shells with the almonds, raisins, and dates for about 30 to 45 seconds. Stir this into the cake batter.

Pour batter into the prepared pan and bake for 35 to 40 minutes or until a cake tester inserted into the center of the cake comes out clean.

In a small saucepan, heat the reserved orange juice with the sugar and brandy until sugar dissolves. While cake is still hot, prick it in several places with a toothpick and spoon the sauce all over it. After about 20 minutes, remove cake from springform and serve.

MAKES ONE 9–INCH CAKE; SERVES 10 TO 12.

Lady Baltimore Cake

Preheat oven to 350 degrees.

Grease and lightly flour three 9 x 2-inch round cake pans. Line the bottoms with waxed paper.

To make the cake: In a large bowl, on the medium speed of an electric mixer, cream the butter and sugar until fluffy, about 3 minutes. Mix the milk and the vanilla and almond extracts together. Add the flour in three parts, alternating with the milk and the vanilla and almond extracts mixture, beating well after each addition.

In a separate bowl, on the high speed of an electric mixer, beat the egg whites until soft peaks form. Gently fold into batter, making sure no streaks of white are showing.

Divide the batter among the prepared pans. Bake for 20 to 25 minutes or until a cake tester inserted into the center of the cake comes out clean. Let cake cool in pans for 10 minutes. Remove from pans and cool completely on wire rack.

To make the filling: In a heavy-bottomed saucepan, whisk the milk with the sugar and flour until thoroughly combined. Cook and stir constantly over medium-high heat (about 5 minutes) until thickened and bubbly. Remove from heat and add the coconut, cookie crumbs, almonds, and cherries. Stir in the vanilla and almond extracts. Cover and cool to room temperature.

When cake has cooled, spread half the filling between the first two layers of cake, then the other half between the second and third layers. The cake should be assembled so it can be iced as soon as the frosting is completed.

To make the frosting: In a standing mixer bowl, combine the egg

CAKE

¾ cup (1½ sticks) unsalted butter, softened

2¼ cups sugar

1½ cups milk

1½ teaspoons vanilla extract

1 teaspoon almond extract

3 cups self-rising flour

6 large egg whites

FILLING

1½ cups milk

1 cup sugar

¼ cup all-purpose flour

2 cups sweetened, shredded coconut

¼ cup apple oatmeal cookie crumbs

¼ cup finely chopped toasted almonds (see Note)

¼ cup quartered maraschino cherries

1 teaspoon vanilla extract

¼ teaspoon almond extract

Lady Baltimore Cake

(continued)

FROSTING

3 large egg whites

1½ teaspoons vanilla extract

½ cup cold water

1½ cups sugar

¼ plus ⅛ teaspoon cream of tartar

GARNISH

Apple-oatmeal cookie crumbs

About 4 maraschino cherries, halved

whites and vanilla and set aside. In a heavy-bottomed saucepan, over high heat, combine the water with the sugar and the cream of tartar. As mixture begins to bubble at the edges, stir once to make sure the sugar is dissolved completely, then let come to a rolling boil (about 2 to 3 minutes) and remove immediately from heat.

Meanwhile, on medium speed, beat the egg whites and the vanilla extract with the whisk attachment until foamy, about 1 minute.

Without turning off the mixer, pour the sugar syrup into the beaten egg whites in a thin, steady stream. Turn the mixer up to medium-high and continue beating constantly for about 5 minutes or until stiff peaks form but frosting is still creamy. Frost top and sides of cake immediately.

Generously sprinkle top with cookie crumbs and place halved cherries on top in a decorative fashion.

MAKES 1 THREE-LAYER 9-INCH CAKE; SERVES 10 TO 12.

★ NOTE: To TOAST ALMONDS, PLACE ON A BAKING SHEET IN A 325-DEGREE OVEN FOR APPROXIMATELY 10 TO 15 MINUTES, OR UNTIL LIGHTLY BROWNED AND FRAGRANT.

Milk Chocolate Layer Cake

Here's a light, delicate cake with just a hint of chocolate flavor—an enormous favorite among my enthusiastic testers. This cake lends itself well to any number of frostings, so take your pick.

Preheat oven to 350 degrees.

Grease and lightly flour two 9 x 2-inch round cake pans. Line the bottoms with waxed paper.

In a medium bowl, sift together the flour, baking powder, and salt. Set aside.

In a large bowl, on the medium speed of an electric mixer, cream the butter and sugar until fluffy, about 3 minutes. Beat in the eggs one at a time. Beat in the melted chocolate, mixing thoroughly. Add in the vanilla and almond extracts. Add the dry ingredients in thirds to the butter mixture, alternating with the milk, beating well after each addition.

Divide the batter between the prepared pans. Bake for 25 to 30 minutes or until a cake tester inserted into the center of the cake comes out clean. Let cake cool in pans for 10 minutes. Remove from pans and cool completely on a wire rack.

When cake has cooled, ice between the layers, then ice top and sides of cake.

MAKES 1 TWO-LAYER 9-INCH CAKE; SERVES 10 TO 12.

★ NOTE: TO MELT CHOCOLATE, PLACE IN A DOUBLE BOILER OVER SIMMERING WATER ON LOW HEAT FOR APPROXIMATELY 5 TO 10 MINUTES. STIR OCCASIONALLY UNTIL COMPLETELY SMOOTH. REMOVE FROM HEAT AND LET COOL FOR 5 TO 10 MINUTES.

2½ cups cake flour

1 tablespoon baking powder

½ teaspoon salt

⅔ cup (1⅓ sticks) unsalted butter, softened

1⅔ cups sugar

3 large eggs, at room temperature

4 ounces milk chocolate, melted (see Note)

2 teaspoons vanilla extract

¼ teaspoon almond extract

1 cup evaporated milk mixed with ½ cup cold water

Orange Marble Pound Cake

> While it's hard to improve upon one of your mom's best cakes,
> I think this comes close as a very suitable equal.
> (Yes, even she approves!)

1½ cups (3 sticks) unsalted butter, softened

3 cups sugar

5 large eggs, at room temperature

3 cups all-purpose flour

¾ cup club soda (not seltzer)

1 tablespoon vanilla extract

2 tablespoons grated orange zest

3 tablespoons orange liqueur

⅓ cup unsweetened cocoa powder

Preheat oven to 350 degrees.

Grease and lightly flour a 10-inch Bundt pan.

In a large bowl, on the medium speed of an electric mixer, cream the butter and sugar until fluffy, about 3 minutes. Add the eggs one at a time, mixing well after each addition. Add the flour in thirds, alternating with the club soda, beating after each addition until smooth. Add the vanilla, zest, and liqueur and mix well.

Pour two-thirds of the batter into the prepared pan. In a small bowl, take the cocoa powder and a few tablespoons of the remaining batter and mix together until smooth. Place this mixture into the pan, pressing it down into the batter. Cover with the remaining batter and bake 1 hour 10 minutes to 1 hour 20 minutes until golden brown, or a cake tester inserted into the center of the cake comes out clean. Let cake cool in pan for 20 minutes. Remove from pan and cool completely on a wire rack.

MAKES ONE 10-INCH CAKE; SERVES 10 TO 12.

To truly "top" this "over the top" cake, try my luscious Classic Chocolate Buttercream (page 111) or sinful Chocolate Whipped Cream Frosting (page 109).

"Over the Top" Chocolate Layer Cake

Preheat oven to 350 degrees.

Grease and lightly flour three 9 x 2-inch round cake pans. Line the bottoms with waxed paper.

In a small bowl, whisk together the cocoa, coffee, and water. Add in the vanilla. Set aside.

In a medium bowl, sift together the flour, baking soda, and salt. Set aside.

In a large bowl, on the medium speed of an electric mixer, cream the butter and sugar until fluffy, about 3 minutes. Beat in the eggs one at a time. Beat in the melted chocolate, mixing thoroughly. Add the dry ingredients in thirds to the butter mixture, alternating with the liquid ingredients, beating well after each addition.

Divide the batter among the prepared pans. Bake for 20 to 25 minutes or until a cake tester inserted into the center of the cake comes out clean. Let cake cool in pans for 10 minutes. Remove from pans and cool completely on wire rack.

If you're making cupcakes, line two 12-cup muffin tins with cupcake papers. Spoon the batter into the cups about three-quarters full. Bake until the tops spring back when lightly touched, about 20 to 22 minutes. Remove cupcakes from pans and cool completely on a rack before icing.

When cake has cooled, ice between the layers, then ice top and sides of cake.

★ NOTE: TO MELT CHOCOLATE, PLACE IN A DOUBLE BOILER OVER SIMMERING WATER ON LOW HEAT FOR APPROXIMATELY 5 TO 10 MINUTES. STIR OCCASIONALLY UNTIL COMPLETELY SMOOTH. REMOVE FROM HEAT AND LET COOL FOR 5 TO 10 MINUTES.

½ cup unsweetened cocoa powder

¾ cup brewed coffee

½ cup cold water

2 teaspoons vanilla extract

2½ cups all-purpose flour

1½ teaspoons baking soda

½ teaspoon salt

¾ cup (1½ sticks) unsalted butter, softened

1½ cups sugar

3 large eggs, at room temperature

6 ounces unsweetened chocolate, melted (see Note)

MAKES 1 THREE–LAYER 9-INCH CAKE OR 24 CUPCAKES; SERVES 10 TO 12.

Pineapple Upside-Down Cake

This moist and yummy cake is classic Americana baking and relatively easy to prepare. Your guests will be surprised at your next luau!

1 cup all-purpose flour

½ teaspoon baking powder

¼ teaspoon salt

2 large eggs, at room temperature

⅔ cup sugar

6 tablespoons pineapple juice (reserved from can)

1 teaspoon vanilla extract

5 tablespoons unsalted butter

½ cup firmly packed light brown sugar

8 pineapple rings (canned in juice, not syrup)

8 whole maraschino cherries (without stems)

About 12 pecan halves

Preheat oven to 350 degrees.

In a small bowl, sift together the flour, baking powder, and salt. Set aside.

In a medium bowl, on the low speed of an electric mixer, beat the eggs with the sugar for about 5 minutes, until thick and lemon-colored. Beat in the juice and the vanilla. Thoroughly beat in the dry ingredients. Set batter aside.

In a large, heavy, ovenproof 10-inch skillet, melt the butter. Sprinkle the brown sugar evenly over the butter. Arrange the drained fruit in an attractive pattern in the pan, placing a cherry in the center of each ring, and the pecan halves all around. Pour the batter over the fruit.

Place the skillet in the oven and bake 40 to 45 minutes, or until a cake tester inserted into the center of the cake comes out clean. Place a serving plate on top of the pan and immediately (and carefully) turn pan upside down. Don't remove the pan for a few minutes to allow the sugar mixture to run down the sides of the cake. Serve warm with whipped cream if desired.

SERVES 4 TO 6.

Sour Cream Spice Cake

This substantial cake always reminds me of whiling away rainy fall afternoons with a cup of tea and a comforting dessert. It's sugar and spice and everything nice, especially topped with Cream Cheese Icing (page 112).

Preheat oven to 350 degrees.

Grease and lightly flour two 9 x 2-inch round cake pans. Line the bottoms with waxed paper.

In a medium bowl, sift together the flour, baking soda, salt, cinnamon, and nutmeg. Set aside.

In a large bowl, on the medium speed of an electric mixer, beat the eggs and sour cream until thoroughly blended, about 1 to 2 minutes. Beat in the brown sugar, mixing thoroughly. Add the dry ingredients and beat until smooth, about 1 to 2 minutes. Add the raisins and nuts.

Divide the batter between the prepared pans. Bake for 25 to 30 minutes or until a cake tester inserted into the center of the cake comes out clean. Let cake cool in pans for 10 minutes. Remove from pans and cool completely on wire rack.

When cake has cooled, ice between the layers, then ice top and sides of cake.

MAKES 1 TWO-LAYER 9-INCH CAKE; SERVES 10 TO 12.

2 cups cake flour

1 teaspoon baking soda

¼ teaspoon salt

2 teaspoons cinnamon

½ teaspoon nutmeg

2 large eggs, at room temperature

1 cup sour cream, at room temperature

2 cups firmly packed light brown sugar

½ cup golden raisins

½ cup chopped walnuts

White Chocolate Layer Cake

½ cup grated white chocolate

½ cup water

2½ cups all-purpose flour

1 teaspoon baking soda

1 cup (2 sticks) unsalted butter, softened

1½ cups sugar

4 large eggs, separated

1 cup buttermilk

1 teaspoon vanilla extract

Preheat oven to 350 degrees.

Grease and lightly flour three 9 x 2-inch round cake pans. Line the bottoms with waxed paper.

In a small saucepan, combine the white chocolate and water and stir over low heat, until chocolate is melted and completely smooth. Set aside.

In a medium bowl, whisk together the flour and baking soda. Set aside.

In a large bowl, on the medium speed of an electric mixer, cream the butter and sugar until fluffy, about 3 minutes. Add in the egg yolks, one at a time. Beat the white chocolate mixture into the batter. Mix the buttermilk and the vanilla extract together. Add the dry ingredients in three parts, alternating with the buttermilk and the vanilla extract mixture, beating well after each addition.

In a separate bowl, on the high speed of an electric mixer, beat the egg whites until soft peaks form. Gently fold into batter, making sure no streaks of white are showing.

Divide the batter among the prepared pans. Bake for 25 to 30 minutes or until a cake tester inserted into the center of the cake comes out clean. Let cake cool in pans for 10 minutes. Remove from pans and cool completely on wire rack.

When cake has cooled, ice between the layers, then ice top and sides of cake.

MAKES 1 THREE-LAYER 9-INCH CAKE; SERVES 10 TO 12.

> *While white cake is usually not too sweet, the chocolate chips add a lovely touch and make it a fun option for a child's birthday party, especially with Peanut Butter Icing (page 117).*

White Layer Cake with Chocolate Chips

Preheat oven to 350 degrees.

Grease and lightly flour two 9 x 2-inch round cake pans. Line the bottoms with waxed paper.

In a medium bowl, sift together the flour, baking powder, and salt. Set aside.

In a large bowl, on the medium speed of an electric mixer, cream the butter and sugar until fluffy, about 3 minutes. Mix the milk and the vanilla extract together. Add the dry ingredients in three parts, alternating with the milk and the vanilla extract mixture, beating well after each addition.

In a separate bowl, on the high speed of an electric mixer, beat the egg whites until soft peaks form. Gently fold into batter, making sure no streaks of white are showing. Then gently stir in the chocolate chips.

Divide the batter between the prepared pans. Bake for 25 to 30 minutes or until a cake tester inserted into the center of the cake comes out clean. Let cake cool in pans for 10 minutes. Remove from pans and cool completely on wire rack.

When cake has cooled, ice between the layers, then ice top and sides of cake.

MAKES 1 TWO–LAYER 9–INCH CAKE; SERVES 10 TO 12.

3 cups cake flour

1 tablespoon baking powder

½ teaspoon salt

⅔ cup (1⅓ sticks) unsalted butter, softened

1¾ cups sugar

1½ cups milk

2 teaspoons vanilla extract

4 large egg whites

1 cup semisweet chocolate chips

Cookies, Bars, and Squares

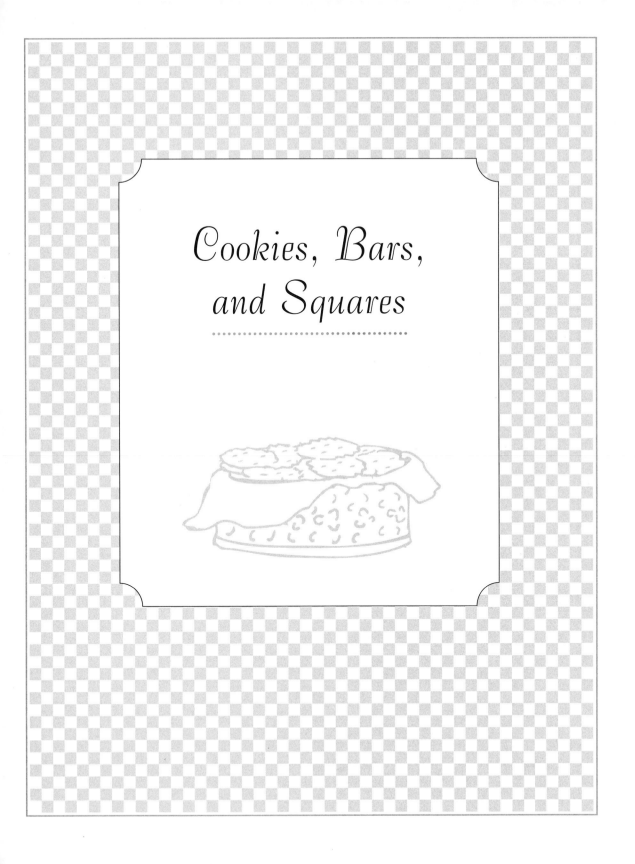

Applesauce Cookies with Dates and Raisins

Preheat oven to 350 degrees.

In a medium bowl, combine the flour and spices. Set aside.

In a large bowl, cream the butter and sugar until fluffy, about 2 to 3 minutes. Add the egg and mix well. Stir the baking soda through the applesauce and add this to the butter mixture. Gradually add the dry ingredients to the butter mixture. Stir in the nuts, dates, and raisins and mix thoroughly.

Drop by rounded teaspoonfuls onto ungreased cookie sheets, leaving several inches between for expansion. Bake for 12 to 14 minutes, or until lightly golden brown. Cool the cookies on the sheets for 1 minute. Remove to a rack to cool completely.

MAKES ABOUT 4 DOZEN COOKIES.

2 cups all-purpose flour

½ teaspoon cinnamon

½ teaspoon ground cloves

½ teaspoon nutmeg

½ cup (1 stick) unsalted butter, softened

1 cup firmly packed light brown sugar

1 large egg, lightly beaten

1 teaspoon baking soda

1 cup unsweetened applesauce

1 cup coarsely chopped walnuts

½ cup chopped dates

½ cup raisins

Chocolate Chip Oatmeal Cookies

Here's a classic cookie that's been raised to new levels—you'll fall in love with them!

¾ cup all-purpose flour

½ teaspoon baking soda

¼ teaspoon salt

½ cup (1 stick) unsalted butter, softened

½ cup sugar

½ cup firmly packed light brown sugar

1 large egg, at room temperature

1 teaspoon vanilla extract

1 cup rolled oats (not quick-cooking oats)

6 ounces semisweet chocolate chips

Preheat oven to 350 degrees.

Lightly grease two or three 12 x 18-inch baking sheets.

In a medium bowl, combine the flour, baking soda, and salt. Set aside.

In a large bowl, cream the butter with the sugars until fluffy, about 2 to 3 minutes. Add the egg and vanilla and mix well. Add the flour mixture and beat thoroughly. Stir in the oats and chocolate chips.

Drop by rounded teaspoonfuls onto prepared cookie sheets, leaving several inches between for expansion. Bake for 10 to 12 minutes, or until lightly golden brown. Cool the cookies on the sheets for 1 minute, then remove to a rack to cool completely.

MAKES 2 TO 3 DOZEN COOKIES.

Chocolate Chunk Macadamia Coconut Cookies

> *This outrageously chocolaty cookie gets the thumbs-up from our most die-hard chocolate lovers.*

Preheat oven to 350 degrees.

In a medium bowl, sift together the flour, cocoa powder, baking soda, and salt. Set aside.

In a large bowl, cream the butter and the sugars until smooth, about 3 minutes. Add the eggs and mix well. Add the chocolate, milk, and vanilla and incorporate thoroughly. Add the dry ingredients and beat well. Stir in the chocolate chunks, nuts, and coconut.

Drop by rounded teaspoonfuls onto ungreased cookie sheets, leaving several inches between for expansion. Bake for 8 to 10 minutes. Cool the cookies on the sheets for 1 minute, then remove to a rack to cool completely.

MAKES 3 TO 4 DOZEN COOKIES.

★ NOTE: TO MELT CHOCOLATE, PLACE IN A DOUBLE BOILER OVER SIMMERING WATER ON LOW HEAT FOR APPROXIMATELY 5 TO 10 MINUTES. STIR OCCASIONALLY UNTIL COMPLETELY SMOOTH. REMOVE FROM HEAT AND LET COOL FOR 5 TO 10 MINUTES.

2½ cups all-purpose flour

½ cup unsweetened cocoa powder

1 teaspoon baking soda

1 teaspoon salt

1⅓ cups (2⅔ sticks) unsalted butter, softened

1 cup sugar

1 cup firmly packed light brown sugar

2 large eggs, at room temperature

2 ounces semisweet chocolate, melted (see Note)

2 tablespoons milk

2 teaspoons vanilla extract

1½ to 2 cups semisweet chocolate chunks

1 cup coarsely chopped macadamia nuts, unsalted

1 cup sweetened, shredded coconut

Cream Cheese Swirl Brownies

> *Love brownies, but don't want to be bowled over by too much chocolate? Then try these swirl brownies, laced with cream cheese filling, to balance out the chocolate. They're heaven!*

BROWNIES

4 ounces semisweet chocolate

5 tablespoons unsalted butter

1 cup sugar

4 large eggs, at room temperature

1 teaspoon vanilla extract

1¼ cups all-purpose flour

1 teaspoon baking powder

¼ teaspoon salt

CREAM CHEESE FILLING

5 tablespoons unsalted butter, softened

8 ounces (1 package) cream cheese, softened

½ cup sugar

2 large eggs, at room temperature

1 teaspoon vanilla extract

Preheat oven to 325 degrees.

Grease and flour a 9 x 13-inch baking pan.

To make the brownies: Melt the chocolate with the butter in a medium saucepan over low heat, stirring occasionally, until smooth. Cool for 5 to 10 minutes. Transfer this mixture to a large bowl and set aside. Meanwhile, prepare the cream cheese filling.

To make the filling: In a large bowl, on the medium speed of an electric mixer, beat the butter and cream cheese for 2 to 3 minutes until smooth. Beat in the sugar and then the eggs, one at a time. Add in the vanilla. Set aside.

Beat the remaining brownie ingredients into the cooled chocolate mixture, in listed order, until smooth. Spread half the chocolate mixture into the prepared pan, then all the cream cheese mixture, then the remaining chocolate mixture. Swirl the chocolate into the cream cheese batter with the tip of a sharp knife to form a decorative pattern.

Bake for 25 to 30 minutes or until a cake tester inserted into the center of the pan comes out clean. Let cool to room temperature before cutting and serving.

MAKES 12 BROWNIES.

Gingersnaps

This sensational cookie is for every spice lover. Add a dash of white pepper for a bit more "bite"; no one will be able to tell what it is.

Preheat oven to 350 degrees.

In a medium bowl, sift together the flour, baking soda, salt, and spices. Set aside.

In a large bowl, cream the butter and brown sugar until fluffy, about 2 to 3 minutes. Add the egg and molasses and mix well. Stir in the vinegar. Add the flour mixture and beat thoroughly.

Drop by rounded teaspoonfuls onto ungreased cookie sheets, leaving several inches between for expansion. Bake for 10 to 12 minutes, or until lightly golden brown. Cool the cookies on the sheets for 1 minute, then remove to a rack to cool completely.

MAKES ABOUT 2 TO 3 DOZEN COOKIES.

2½ cups all-purpose flour

2 teaspoons baking soda

½ teaspoon salt

1 teaspoon ground ginger

½ teaspoon cinnamon

½ teaspoon nutmeg

⅛ teaspoon ground white pepper (optional)

6 tablespoons (¾ stick) unsalted butter, softened

1 cup firmly packed light brown sugar

1 large egg, at room temperature

¼ cup light unsulfured molasses

1 teaspoon distilled white vinegar

Hermits

There are many versions of this cookie, dating back to the early settlers. These supposedly kept well on ships, which is why they were so popular. They will be with you, too, so make sure to keep plenty of these stowaways on hand!

1 ½ cups all-purpose flour

½ teaspoon baking powder

¼ teaspoon salt

½ teaspoon cinnamon

¼ teaspoon allspice

¼ teaspoon ground ginger

¼ teaspoon nutmeg

½ cup (1 stick) unsalted
   butter, softened

1 cup firmly packed light
   brown sugar

2 large eggs, at room
   temperature

1 cup chopped golden raisins

½ cup finely chopped
   blanched almonds

Preheat oven to 350 degrees.

In a medium bowl, sift together the flour, baking powder, salt, and spices. Set aside.

In a large bowl, cream the butter and brown sugar until fluffy, about 2 to 3 minutes. Add the eggs one at a time and mix well. Add the flour mixture and beat thoroughly. Stir in the raisins and nuts.

Drop by rounded teaspoonfuls onto ungreased cookie sheets, leaving several inches between for expansion. Bake for 8 to 10 minutes, or until lightly golden brown. Cool the cookies on the sheets for 1 minute, then remove to a rack to cool completely.

MAKES ABOUT 3 DOZEN COOKIES.

Lemon Meringue Bars

These bars may be time-consuming to prepare, but they are well worth the effort. They pack all the succulent flavors and textures of a lemon meringue pie into a three-inch bar.

Preheat oven to 350 degrees.

Lightly grease a 9 x 13-inch baking pan.

To make the crust: In a medium bowl, on the low speed of an electric mixer, combine all the ingredients until mixture resembles coarse crumbs. Form the dough into a ball. Spread crust evenly into the prepared pan. Use a large piece of waxed paper to firmly and evenly press down crust.

Bake the crust for 18 to 20 minutes until lightly golden. Remove from oven and let cool for 15 to 20 minutes before proceeding.

While the crust is cooling, make the topping: In a medium bowl, on the low speed of an electric mixer, beat the sugar, eggs, lemon juice, and zest until well combined. Pour over slightly warm crust.

Return crust to oven. Bake 18 to 20 minutes until edges are golden brown.

While the bars are baking, in a small bowl on the high speed of an electric mixer, beat the egg whites and the sugar until soft and glossy, about 3 minutes.

Remove the bars from oven and add the meringue, spreading it carefully over the entire surface with a rubber spatula.

Return to oven a third time, and bake another 10 to 12 minutes until meringue is golden brown and firm. Allow to cool to room temperature before cutting and serving.

MAKES TWELVE 3-INCH BARS.

CRUST
1 cup (2 sticks) unsalted butter, softened
2 cups all-purpose flour
½ cup confectioners' sugar
¼ teaspoon salt
1 teaspoon grated lemon zest

LEMON TOPPING
1 cup sugar
3 large eggs, at room temperature
½ cup lemon juice
3 teaspoons grated lemon zest

MERINGUE TOPPING
4 large egg whites
½ cup sugar

Oatmeal Butterscotch Cookies

These cookies aren't your standard oatmeal cookie—the addition of butterscotch chips gives a depth of flavor and sweetness to this classic.

1¼ cups all-purpose flour

1 teaspoon baking soda

¼ teaspoon salt

¾ cup (1½ sticks) unsalted butter, softened

¾ cup sugar

¾ cup firmly packed light brown sugar

2 large eggs, at room temperature

1 teaspoon vanilla extract

3 cups rolled oats (not quick-cooking oats)

1½ cups (1 10-ounce package) butterscotch chips

Preheat oven to 350 degrees.

Lightly grease two or three 12 x 18-inch baking sheets.

In a medium bowl, whisk together the flour, baking soda, and salt. Set aside.

In a large bowl, cream the butter with the sugars until fluffy, about 2 to 3 minutes. Add the eggs, one at a time, and mix well. Add the vanilla. Add in the flour mixture and beat thoroughly. Stir in the oats and the chips until well incorporated.

Drop by rounded teaspoonfuls onto the prepared cookie sheets, leaving several inches between for expansion. Bake for 10 to 12 minutes or until lightly golden. Cool cookies on the sheets for 1 minute, then remove to a rack to cool completely.

MAKES ABOUT 3 TO 4 DOZEN COOKIES.

Oreo Brownies

Although not technically a brownie, this toothsome, gooey bar is perfect for a small snack or the school bake sale. You'll want to cut them small because they pack a lot of sweetness.

Preheat oven to 350 degrees.

Line an 8 x 8-inch baking pan with aluminum foil, leaving an overhang of foil around the edges. Lightly grease the pan.

In a large bowl, mix the cookies with the butter. Pour half the mixture into the prepared pan. Sprinkle with the chips, marshmallows, and walnuts. Top with the remaining cookie mixture. Pour the milk evenly over the surface of the pan.

Bake for 28 to 32 minutes, or until lightly golden. Let cool to room temperature and lift the bars from the pan. Peel back the foil and cut into serving pieces.

MAKES ABOUT SIXTEEN 2-INCH BARS.

26 to 28 chocolate sandwich cookies, coarsely chopped

2 tablespoons unsalted butter, melted

½ cup semisweet chocolate chips

½ cup vanilla chips or white chocolate chips

¾ cup mini-marshmallows

½ cup coarsely chopped walnuts

1 (14-ounce) can sweetened condensed milk

Peanut Butter Heath Bar Pecan Cookies

My feeling is that you can never go wrong eating a dessert containing peanut butter. I'm sure you'll agree after you taste these cookies.

1½ cups all-purpose flour

½ teaspoon baking powder

½ teaspoon baking soda

¼ teaspoon salt

½ cup (1 stick) unsalted butter, softened

½ cup chunky peanut butter

¼ cup firmly packed light brown sugar

¾ cup sugar

2 large eggs, at room temperature

1 teaspoon vanilla extract

1½ to 2 cups coarsely chopped mini–Heath bars

½ cup coarsely chopped pecans

Preheat oven to 350 degrees.

In a medium bowl, sift together the flour, baking powder, baking soda, and salt. Set aside.

In a large bowl, cream the butter and peanut butter until smooth, about 1 to 2 minutes. Gradually add the sugars and beat another 2 minutes. Add the eggs and vanilla and mix well. Add the dry ingredients and thoroughly incorporate. Stir in the Heath bars and nuts.

Drop by rounded teaspoonfuls onto ungreased cookie sheets, leaving several inches between for expansion. Bake for 12 to 14 minutes, or until lightly golden. Cool the cookies on the sheets for 1 minute, then remove to a rack to cool completely.

MAKES ABOUT 5 DOZEN COOKIES.

An enormous favorite at the bakery, this chewy cookielike bar combines so many delicious flavors, your sweet tooth won't know where to begin.

Preheat oven to 325 degrees.

Grease and lightly flour a 9 x 13-inch baking pan.

In a medium bowl, whisk together the flour, baking soda, and salt. Set aside.

In a large bowl, on the low speed of an electric mixer, cream the butter and sugar until fluffy, about 2 to 3 minutes. Beat in the peanut butter until well mixed. Add the egg and vanilla. Add the dry ingredients to the butter mixture and incorporate thoroughly. Stir in ½ cup of the chocolate chips, the vanilla chips, ¼ cup of the peanut butter chips, and the nuts. Spread mixture evenly into prepared pan.

Bake for 25 to 30 minutes. Remove from oven and immediately sprinkle on the remaining ¼ cup chocolate chips and ¼ cup peanut butter chips. Allow to sit for a minute or so. Smooth out the chips with a rubber spatula as they begin to melt.

Cool for 20 minutes or so before sprinkling the topping chips evenly over the surface. Let cool completely before cutting and serving.

MAKES TWELVE 5-INCH BARS.

Bar

1 cup all-purpose flour

½ teaspoon baking soda

¼ teaspoon salt

½ cup (1 stick) unsalted butter, softened

1 cup firmly packed light brown sugar

½ cup creamy peanut butter

1 large egg, at room temperature

1 teaspoon vanilla extract

¾ cup chocolate chips

¼ cup vanilla chips or white chocolate chips

½ cup peanut butter chips

¼ cup coarsely chopped pecans

Topping

2 tablespoons chocolate chips

2 tablespoons vanilla chips or white chocolate chips

2 tablespoons peanut butter chips

Rice Krispies Treats

A simple nostalgic treat from childhood—a perfect snack when something light and not too sweet is in order. This is a great, no-bake recipe to make with children.

2 tablespoons unsalted butter

4½ cups mini-marshmallows

6 cups Rice Krispies cereal

Generously grease a 9 x 13-inch baking pan.

In a heavy-bottomed saucepan, melt the butter and then stir in the marshmallows. Stir until melted and smooth. Pour this into a large bowl, and mix in the cereal until well combined. Transfer to the prepared pan and press mixture down evenly. Allow 5 minutes before cutting and serving.

MAKES TWELVE 3-INCH SQUARES.

The Greatest Brownies Ever

Every cookbook claims to have discovered the "greatest brownie recipe ever" and this book is no different! These rich and chocolaty brownies are offered at Buttercup with or without walnuts, and both varieties practically fly out the door!

Preheat oven to 350 degrees.

Grease and lightly flour a 9 x 13-inch baking pan.

In a medium bowl, sift together the flour, baking powder, and salt. Set aside.

In a medium saucepan over low heat, melt the chocolate with the butter, stirring occasionally, until smooth. Cool for 20 minutes.

Transfer this mixture to a large bowl and, with a wooden spoon, mix in the sugar, eggs, espresso powder, and vanilla and rum extracts. Add the dry ingredients and mix thoroughly.

Pour the batter into the prepared pan. Bake for 25 to 30 minutes, or until a cake tester inserted into the center of the pan comes out with moist crumbs attached. Do not overbake. Allow to cool to room temperature (or preferably overnight) before cutting and serving.

VARIATION: TOP WITH COARSELY CHOPPED WALNUTS BEFORE BAKING.

MAKES TWELVE 3-INCH BROWNIES.

½ cup all-purpose flour

1½ teaspoons baking powder

½ teaspoon salt

1⅓ cups semisweet chocolate chips

3 ounces unsweetened chocolate

1 cup (2 sticks) unsalted butter

1 cup sugar

3 large eggs, at room temperature

1 tablespoon instant espresso powder

1 tablespoon vanilla extract

¼ teaspoon rum extract

Thumbprint Cookies

What's great about this recipe is that the dough can be made in advance and refrigerated for later use. Terrific filled with jam (or citrus curd), these are also perfect for holiday cookie sessions with the kids.

2 cups all-purpose flour

2 teaspoons baking powder

1 cup (2 sticks) unsalted
   butter, softened

1 cup sugar

1 large egg, at room
   temperature

1 teaspoon vanilla extract

¼ cup milk

Jelly, jam, or citrus curd of
   your choice for filling

Preheat oven to 350 degrees.

Lightly grease two or three 12 x 18-inch baking sheets.

In a medium bowl, combine the flour and baking powder. Set aside.

In a large bowl, cream the butter and sugar until fluffy, about 2 to 3 minutes. Add the egg and vanilla and mix well. Add the flour mixture alternating with the milk and beat thoroughly. If dough is very soft and sticky, refrigerate for 10 minutes or so before proceeding.

Drop rounded teaspoonfuls onto prepared cookie sheets, leaving several inches between for expansion. Make an indentation in the center of each cookie with your thumb and fill with your favorite jam or citrus curd. Bake for 10 to 12 minutes, or until lightly golden. Cool cookies on the sheets for 1 minute, then remove to a rack to cool completely.

MAKES ABOUT 5½ DOZEN COOKIES.

Pies, Crisps, and Cobblers

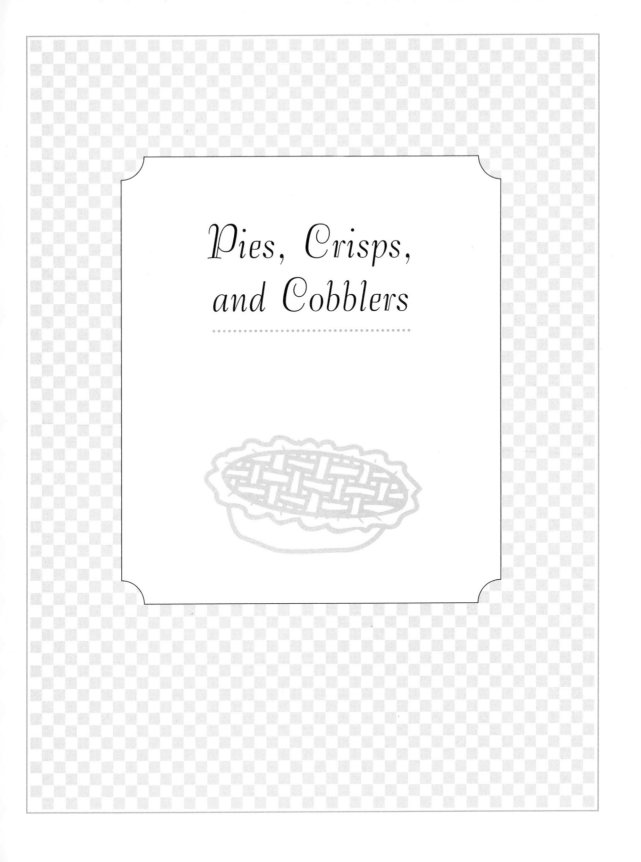

Apple Butter Apple Pie

To take the classic apple pie one step further, I've added apple butter for an even juicier and more scrumptious treat.

Preheat oven to 425 degrees.

To make the crust: Place the flour, sugar, and salt in a large bowl and, using a pastry blender, cut in the butter until the mixture resembles coarse cornmeal. Sprinkle the ice water by tablespoons over the flour mixture, tossing with a fork until all of the dough is moistened. Form the dough into a ball. On a lightly floured surface, roll out the dough to fit into a 9-inch glass pie dish. Fold the edges under all around the rim and crimp.

To prepare the filling: Combine the flour, sugar, and spices. Add the apple slices, apple butter, and lemon juice and gently toss until coated. Transfer the apple mixture into the piecrust.

To prepare the topping: Mix together the flour, brown sugar, oats, and cinnamon. Using a pastry blender, cut in the butter until the mixture resembles coarse crumbs.

Sprinkle the crumb topping over the apple mixture until well covered. Bake at 425 degrees for 10 minutes. Turn down the oven to 350 degrees and continue baking for an additional 25 to 35 minutes, or until crumbs are golden brown. Remove from oven and let pie cool on a rack for at least 30 minutes before serving.

MAKES ONE 9-INCH PIE; SERVES 6 TO 8.

CRUST

1½ cups all-purpose flour

1 tablespoon sugar

¼ teaspoon salt

½ cup (1 stick) cold unsalted butter, cut into small pieces

2 to 3 tablespoons ice water

FILLING

1½ tablespoons all-purpose flour

⅜ cup sugar

¼ teaspoon cinnamon

Pinch of nutmeg

3 cups peeled, cored, and sliced tart apples, such as Granny Smith or pippins

¼ cup apple butter

1 tablespoon lemon juice

TOPPING

1 cup all-purpose flour

⅔ cup firmly packed light brown sugar

1 cup rolled oats (not quick-cooking oats)

¼ teaspoon cinnamon

10 tablespoons (1¼ sticks) unsalted butter, softened

Apple Cobbler

Here's an old-fashioned midwestern cobbler that will satisfy your taste buds every time.

FILLING

4 cups peeled, cored, and thinly sliced apples, such as Golden Delicious or pippins

½ cup firmly packed light brown sugar

¼ teaspoon almond extract

½ teaspoon cinnamon

½ teaspoon nutmeg

2 tablespoons unsalted butter, cut into small pieces

CRUST

1 cup all-purpose flour

4 tablespoons sugar

2 teaspoons baking powder

¼ teaspoon salt

4 tablespoons vegetable shortening

6 tablespoons milk

Preheat oven to 400 degrees.

Arrange the apples in the bottom of a greased 8-inch deep-dish baking pan. Combine the brown sugar, almond extract, and spices and sprinkle over the apples. Dot with the butter and set aside.

In a large bowl, combine the flour, sugar, baking powder, and salt. Using a pastry blender (or two forks), cut in the shortening. Pour in the milk slowly and stir until just mixed, stirring constantly with a fork. Add more droplets of milk if dough is dry. Gather the dough into a ball and place on a floured surface. Sprinkle with flour if necessary to make dough less sticky. Roll with a rolling pin to a ½-inch thickness.

Spread the dough over the apples and bake 35 to 40 minutes, or until juices are bubbling and the crust is golden brown. Serve warm with whipped cream if desired.

MAKES 1 COBBLER; SERVES 6 TO 8.

Butterscotch Pie

This smooth-as-silk pie recipe is tough to beat for the butterscotch lover. Don't be scared of the consistency while cooking, it'll work itself out and produce a lovely confection.

Preheat oven to 400 degrees.

To make the crust: Place the flour, sugar, and salt in a large bowl and, using a pastry blender, cut in the butter until the mixture resembles coarse cornmeal. Sprinkle the ice water by tablespoons over the flour mixture, tossing with a fork until all of the dough is moistened. Form the dough into a ball. On a lightly floured surface, roll out the dough to fit into a 9-inch glass pie dish. Fold the edges under all around the rim and crimp.

Cover the shell with foil and line the foil with pie weights. Bake for 10 minutes. Remove from oven and carefully take out the weights and the foil. Cool on a wire rack for 10 minutes.

To prepare the filling: In a heavy-bottomed saucepan, melt 4 tablespoons of the butter and then pour in the brown sugar. Cook and stir over low heat for 2 minutes, until bubbly. Remove from heat and set aside.

Place the salt and cornstarch in a bowl along with the egg yolks and 4 tablespoons of the milk. Whisk until the cornstarch is dissolved. Stir in the remaining milk. Bring the brown sugar mixture back to a boil and pour in the egg mixture. Cook over medium heat, stirring constantly, until it boils. (The brown sugar mixture will be lumpy and candylike. Don't worry, it will dissolve as it cooks.) Reduce heat and cook 3 minutes more. Remove from heat and add the remaining butter and the vanilla, mixing thoroughly. Place a piece of plastic wrap directly on the filling and let cool for about 15 minutes. Remove the plastic, stir the filling completely, and pour into the prepared pie shell. Allow pie to cool for 30 minutes, then refrigerate for at least 2 hours before serving.

CRUST

1½ cups all-purpose flour

1 tablespoon sugar

¼ teaspoon salt

½ cup (1 stick) cold unsalted butter, cut into small pieces

2 to 3 tablespoons ice water

FILLING

6 tablespoons (¾ stick) unsalted butter

1 cup firmly packed light brown sugar

¼ teaspoon salt

4 tablespoons cornstarch

4 large egg yolks, lightly beaten

3 cups milk

1 teaspoon vanilla extract

MAKES ONE 9-INCH PIE;

SERVES 6 TO 8.

Chocolate Peanut Butter Mud Pie

CRUST

6 tablespoons (¾ stick) unsalted butter, melted

2 cups chocolate wafer crumbs

2 tablespoons sugar

FILLING

12 ounces (1½ packages) cream cheese, softened

¾ cup confectioners' sugar

1 cup creamy peanut butter

1 tablespoon vanilla extract

1 cup heavy cream

1 cup coarsely chopped peanut butter cups

GARNISH

¾ cup semisweet chocolate chips

2 tablespoons heavy cream

½ cup coarsely chopped unsalted peanuts

½ cup (or more) coarsely chopped peanut butter cups

To make the crust: Combine the butter, cookie crumbs, and sugar and press firmly into a lightly buttered 9-inch deep-dish pie pan or casserole. Wrap tightly with plastic and place in the freezer for 30 minutes.

To prepare the filling: Place the cream cheese and sugar in a medium bowl and, on the low speed of an electric mixer, beat until smooth. Add the peanut butter and vanilla and beat until combined.

In a separate bowl, whip the cream until soft peaks are formed. Gently fold in half of the whipped cream, then the other half until just combined. Fold in the peanut butter cups. Spoon into the prepared crust. Cover and refrigerate for 2 hours.

To prepare the topping: In a small saucepan, melt the chocolate chips with the cream and stir until smooth. Let cool for 10 minutes. Drizzle the sauce over the pie in a decorative fashion. Sprinkle the peanuts and peanut butter cups over the top and refrigerate for 1 hour.

MAKES ONE 9-INCH PIE; SERVES 6 TO 8.

Substitute fresh nectarines if you like. I love to serve this with a side of vanilla ice cream dotted with fresh blueberries.

CRUST

1½ cups all-purpose flour

1 tablespoon sugar

¼ teaspoon salt

½ cup (1 stick) cold unsalted butter, cut into small pieces

2 to 3 tablespoons ice water

FILLING

5 tablespoons all-purpose flour

¾ cup sugar

¼ teaspoon salt

½ teaspoon ground ginger

5 to 6 cups peeled, pitted, and sliced peaches (drop peaches in boiling water for 1 minute, then plunge into cold water to peel more easily)

2 tablespoons lemon juice

2 tablespoons unsalted butter

TOPPING

1 cup all-purpose flour

⅔ cup firmly packed light brown sugar

1 cup rolled oats (not quick-cooking oats)

¼ teaspoon cinnamon

10 tablespoons (1¼ sticks) unsalted butter, softened

Preheat oven to 425 degrees.

To make the crust: Place the flour, sugar, and salt in a large bowl and, using a pastry blender, cut in the butter until the mixture resembles coarse cornmeal. Sprinkle the ice water by tablespoons over the flour mixture, tossing with a fork until all of the dough is moistened. Form dough into a ball. On a lightly floured surface, roll out the dough to fit into a 9-inch glass pie dish. Fold the edges under all around the rim and crimp.

To prepare the filling: Place the flour, sugar, salt, and ginger in a bowl and whisk to combine. Stir in the fruit, pour in the lemon juice, and gently toss until coated. Transfer this mixture into the piecrust and dot with slices of butter.

To prepare the topping: Mix together the flour, brown sugar, oats, and cinnamon. Using a pastry blender, cut in the butter until the mixture resembles coarse crumbs.

Sprinkle the crumb topping over the fruit mixture until well covered.

Bake at 425 degrees for 10 minutes. Turn down the oven to 350 degrees and continue baking for an additional 25 to 35 minutes, or until crumbs are golden brown. Remove from oven and let pie cool on rack for at least 30 minutes before serving.

MAKES ONE 9-INCH PIE; SERVES 6 TO 8.

German Chocolate Pie

CRUST

½ cup (1 stick) unsalted butter, melted

2 cups graham cracker crumbs

2 tablespoons sugar

FILLING

1 package (4 ounces) Baker's German's Sweet Baking Chocolate, broken into squares

4 tablespoons (½ stick) unsalted butter

1⅔ cups evaporated milk

1½ cups sugar

1 tablespoon cornstarch

½ teaspoon salt

2 large eggs, at room temperature

1 teaspoon vanilla extract

1½ cups sweetened, shredded coconut

½ cup finely chopped pecans

Preheat oven to 375 degrees.

To make the crust: Combine the butter with the graham cracker crumbs and the sugar. Press firmly into a lightly buttered 9-inch glass pie dish. Place on a baking sheet and bake for 10 minutes.

To make the filling: In a medium saucepan, melt the chocolate with the butter, stirring until smooth. Remove from heat and slowly blend in the evaporated milk. In a small bowl, mix the sugar, cornstarch, and salt. Beat in the eggs and the vanilla and slowly blend this into the chocolate mixture. Pour the mixture into the prepared pie shell. Sprinkle the coconut and the pecans on top. Bake for 40 to 45 minutes, or until set and lightly golden. Allow pie to cool for about 30 minutes. Refrigerate until completely cold, at least 1 hour.

MAKES ONE 9-INCH PIE; SERVES 6 TO 8.

Lemon Meringue Pie

Preheat oven to 400 degrees.

To make the crust: Place the flour, sugar, and salt in a large bowl and, using a pastry blender, cut in the butter until the mixture resembles coarse cornmeal. Sprinkle the ice water by tablespoons over the flour mixture, tossing with a fork until all of the dough is moistened. Form dough into a ball. On a lightly floured surface, roll out the dough to fit into a 9-inch glass pie dish. Fold the edges under all around the rim and crimp.

Cover the shell with foil and line the foil with pie weights. Bake for 10 minutes. Remove from oven and carefully take out the weights and the foil. Cool on a wire rack for 10 minutes.

To prepare the filling: Whisk the egg yolks in a small bowl until lemony in color. Set aside.

In a heavy-bottomed saucepan on medium heat, place the sugar, cornstarch, and water. Stir constantly until thick. Boil this for 1 minute.

Pour half of the above mixture into the egg yolks and whisk to combine. Pour this back into the pot containing the remaining half. Boil for 1 minute more, stirring constantly. Remove from heat and stir until smooth. Blend into the saucepan the butter, lemon juice, and zest. Stir until smooth. Pour filling into the prepared pie shell.

For the meringue: In a small bowl, on the high speed of an electric mixer, whip the egg whites for 1 to 2 minutes. Add in the sugar gradually, and whip until whites are thick and glossy, about another 1 to 2 minutes.

Cover filling generously with the meringue, swirling into peaks with a small rubber spatula. Bake 15 to 18 minutes, until lightly browned.

Allow pie to cool for 1 hour. Refrigerate until completely cold, at least 1 hour.

MAKES ONE 9-INCH PIE; SERVES 6 TO 8.

CRUST
1½ cups all-purpose flour
1 tablespoon sugar
¼ teaspoon salt
½ cup (1 stick) cold unsalted butter, cut into small pieces
2 to 3 tablespoons ice water

FILLING
3 large egg yolks
1½ cups sugar
⅓ cup cornstarch
1½ cups water
3 tablespoons unsalted butter
6 tablespoons lemon juice
3 tablespoons lemon zest

MERINGUE TOPPING
4 large egg whites
½ cup sugar

Mom's Summer Icebox Pie

My mother always makes this in the summer for barbecues and other informal meals. It takes 5 minutes to prepare, and the results are out of this world! Choose any flavors of yogurt you like to mix together (my favorites are peach and boysenberry).

CRUST

4 tablespoons (½ stick) unsalted butter, melted

1½ cups gingersnap or graham cracker cookie crumbs

FILLING

1 (8-ounce) container Cool Whip

2 (8-ounce) containers fruit yogurt

1 cup diced fresh peaches or summer fruit of choice such as raspberries, blueberries, or plums

To make the crust: Combine the butter and cookie crumbs and press firmly into a lightly buttered 9-inch glass pie dish. Wrap tightly with plastic and place in the freezer for 30 minutes.

To make the filling: Thoroughly mix together the whipped topping and the yogurt in a large bowl. Toss in desired fresh fruit. Pour into the prepared pie shell and place in the freezer, covered, for at least 6 hours. Allow the pie to thaw to room temperature for no more than 10 minutes before serving.

MAKES ONE 9-INCH PIE; SERVES 4 TO 6.

Lady Baltimore Cake

White Fudge with Walnuts and Dried Cranberries, Hermits,
Peanut Butter Heath Bar Pecan Cookies

Red Velvet Cake

Raspberry Cream Cheese Buns, Whole Wheat Maple
Syrup Muffins, Orange Glazed Muffins

Lemon Meringue Pie

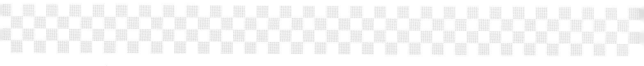

Orange Marble Pound Cake

Banana Pudding with Nilla Wafers

Buttercup Golden Layer Cake

Old-Fashioned Buttermilk Pie

While this pie can be made with a standard pastry crust, I like it with a cereal crumb crust for the perfect breakfast pie. Be sure to refrigerate leftovers, but there might not be any. . . .

Preheat oven to 425 degrees.

To make the crust: Combine the butter with the cereal crumbs and sugar. Press firmly into a 9-inch glass pie dish and bake for 8 minutes. Remove from oven and cool on rack for 10 minutes.

To prepare the filling: Whisk together the sugar and the flour. Add in the remaining ingredients and stir until well blended. Pour into the pie shell and bake at 425 degrees for 10 minutes, then turn down the oven to 350 degrees and bake for 30 to 35 minutes more. When done, filling will be puffy and a bit jiggly. Remove from oven and let pie cool on a rack for at least 30 minutes. Serve slightly warm.

MAKES ONE 9-INCH PIE; SERVES 6 TO 8.

CRUST

6 tablespoons (¾ stick) unsalted butter, melted

1½ cups cornflake crumbs

¼ cup sugar

FILLING

1 cup sugar

3 tablespoons all-purpose flour

3 large eggs, well beaten

½ cup (1 stick) unsalted butter, melted

1 cup buttermilk

3 tablespoons lemon juice

1 tablespoon lemon zest

Pear Crisp

A perfect autumn dessert. You can substitute apples if you like, or add in a few cranberries for some extra tartness.

CRISP

4 cups peeled, cored, and
   sliced pears (about 4
   medium Bosc pears)

¼ cup water

1 teaspoon lemon zest

1 teaspoon cinnamon

¼ teaspoon nutmeg

TOPPING

¾ cup all-purpose flour

½ cup sugar

½ cup firmly packed light
   brown sugar

½ cup (1 stick) unsalted
   butter, softened

Preheat oven to 350 degrees.

For the crisp: Toss the pears with the water, zest, and spices. Arrange the fruit in the bottom of a greased 8-inch deep-dish baking pan.

To prepare the topping: Mix together the flour and the sugars. Using a pastry blender, cut in the butter until the mixture resembles coarse crumbs. Sprinkle evenly over the fruit and bake for 40 to 45 minutes, or until juices are bubbling and the crumbs are lightly golden. Serve warm with whipped cream if desired.

MAKES 1 CRISP; SERVES 6 TO 8.

Strawberry Rhubarb Pie

A light, warm breeze, sitting on the porch with friends, and a slice of strawberry rhubarb pie are the perfect ingredients for a lovely summer evening.

Preheat oven to 425 degrees.

To make the crust: Place the flour, sugar, and salt in a large bowl and, using a pastry blender, cut in the butter until the mixture resembles coarse cornmeal. Sprinkle the ice water by tablespoons over the flour mixture, tossing with a fork until all of the dough is moistened. Form dough into a ball. On a lightly floured surface, roll out the dough to fit into a 9-inch glass pie dish. Fold the edges under all around the rim and crimp.

To prepare the filling: Beat the eggs until lemony in color. Add in the sugar, flour, and spices. Stir in the fruit and gently toss until coated. Transfer this into the piecrust and dot with slices of butter.

To prepare the topping: Mix together the flour, brown sugar, oats, and cinnamon. Using a pastry blender, cut in the butter until the mixture resembles coarse crumbs.

Sprinkle the crumb topping over the fruit mixture until well covered. Bake at 425 degrees for 10 minutes, then turn down the oven to 350 degrees and continue baking for an additional 25 to 35 minutes, or until crumbs are golden brown. Remove from oven and let pie cool on rack for at least 30 minutes before serving.

MAKES ONE 9-INCH PIE; SERVES 6 TO 8.

CRUST

1½ cups all-purpose flour

1 tablespoon sugar

¼ teaspoon salt

½ cup (1 stick) cold unsalted butter, cut into small pieces

2 to 3 tablespoons ice water

FILLING

2 large eggs, at room temperature

1½ cups sugar

3 tablespoons all-purpose flour

½ teaspoon cinnamon

¼ teaspoon nutmeg

1½ cups rhubarb, cut into ½-inch pieces

1½ cups sliced strawberries

2 tablespoons unsalted butter, cut into small pieces

TOPPING

1 cup all-purpose flour

⅔ cup firmly packed light brown sugar

1 cup rolled oats (not quick-cooking oats)

¼ teaspoon cinnamon

10 tablespoons (1¼ sticks) unsalted butter, softened

Two-Crust Cherry Pie

Since I find it so time-consuming to pit cherries, here's a terrific recipe using canned fruit. Sour cherries make the best pie if you can find them. I like to make this pie with a double crust.

PIE DOUGH FOR
DOUBLE CRUST

3 cups all-purpose flour

2 tablespoons sugar

½ teaspoon salt

1 cup (2 sticks) cold unsalted
   butter, cut into small
   pieces

4 to 5 tablespoons ice water
   (a bit more if needed)

FILLING

½ cup sugar

3 tablespoons all-purpose
   flour

4 cups canned cherries, well
   drained

2 tablespoons unsalted butter,
   cut into small pieces

Preheat oven to 425 degrees.

To make the crust: Place the flour, sugar, and salt in a large bowl and, using a pastry blender, cut in the butter until the mixture resembles coarse cornmeal. Sprinkle the ice water by tablespoons over the flour mixture, tossing with a fork until all of the dough is moistened. Form dough into a ball.

On a lightly floured surface, roll out half the dough to fit into a 9-inch glass pie dish. Fold the edges under all around the rim and crimp. Roll out the remaining dough and set it aside on a piece of waxed paper or lightly floured surface.

To prepare the filling: Combine the sugar and flour and whisk to combine. Stir in the fruit and gently toss until coated. Transfer this into the piecrust and dot with slices of butter. Moisten edges of bottom crust and press top crust down. Trim top pastry with a knife, and fold the edges underneath. Press edges with the tines of a fork.

Bake at 425 degrees for 25 minutes, until juices are bubbling and crust has begun to brown. Reduce heat to 350 degrees and bake for another 20 to 25 minutes, until top is well browned. Remove from oven and let pie cool on a rack for at least 30 minutes before serving.

MAKES ONE 9-INCH PIE; SERVES 6 TO 8.

The Breakfast Basket ★ Quick Breads, Biscuits, Coffee Cakes, Buns, and Muffins

Apple Berry Muffins

This is a tasty (and believe it or not) fat-free muffin. I like raspberries in mine, but use cranberries if you like a more tart flavor.

Preheat oven to 375 degrees. Generously grease a 12-cup muffin tin.

In a large bowl, mix the dry ingredients, making a well in the center. Stir in the liquid ingredients until just combined, being careful not to overmix. Batter may be lumpy. Gently fold the berries and the apples into the batter.

Fill the muffin cups about three-quarters full. Lightly sprinkle each muffin with sugar.

Bake for 18 to 22 minutes until lightly golden, or until a cake tester inserted into the center of muffin comes out with moist crumbs attached. Do not overbake.

MAKES 12 MUFFINS.

2 cups whole wheat flour
1 tablespoon baking powder
1 1/4 cups unsweetened applesauce
1/2 cup maple syrup
2 large egg whites, lightly beaten
1/2 cup raspberries (or other berries)
1/2 cup peeled, chopped apples
1 tablespoon sugar (for sprinkling)

Banana Nut Quick Bread

1 cup all-purpose flour

1 teaspoon baking soda

¼ teaspoon salt

½ teaspoon nutmeg

½ cup (1 stick) unsalted butter, softened

½ cup sugar

2 large eggs, at room temperature

½ cup whole wheat flour

3 large ripe bananas, mashed or pureed

1 teaspoon vanilla extract

½ cup finely chopped walnuts

Preheat oven to 350 degrees.

Grease and lightly flour a 9 x 5 x 3-inch loaf pan.

In a medium bowl, sift together the flour, baking soda, salt, and nutmeg. Set aside.

In a large bowl, cream the butter and sugar until fluffy, about 2 to 3 minutes. Add the eggs one at a time. Add in the sifted dry ingredients, and then the whole wheat flour, mixing well. Thoroughly mix in the bananas, vanilla, and nuts.

Pour the batter into the prepared pan and bake for 50 to 60 minutes, or until a cake tester inserted into the center of the loaf comes out clean. Let cool for 20 minutes before serving.

MAKES 1 LOAF; SERVES 8 TO 10.

Blueberry Coffee Cake

Preheat oven to 350 degrees.

Grease and flour a 9 x 13-inch baking pan.

To make the cake: In a medium bowl, sift together the flour, baking powder, and salt. Set aside.

In a small bowl, coat the blueberries in the 2 tablespoons of remaining flour. Set aside.

In a large bowl, on the medium speed of an electric mixer, cream the butter and shortening until smooth, about 2 minutes. Gradually add the sugar and continue beating another 2 minutes. Add the eggs until well incorporated. Mix the milk and almond extract together. Add the dry ingredients in thirds, alternating with the milk and almond extract mixture, beating well after each addition. Fold in the coated blueberries.

To make the topping: In a medium bowl, on the low speed of an electric mixer, cream the shortening with the sugar for about 1 to 2 minutes. Mix in the flour and cinnamon until the mixture resembles coarse crumbs.

Pour the batter into the prepared pan and sprinkle the crumb topping over the batter until well covered. Bake for 40 to 50 minutes, or until a cake tester inserted into the center of the cake comes out with moist crumbs attached.

Let cool for 20 minutes before serving.

MAKES 1 CAKE.

CAKE

4 cups all-purpose flour plus 2 tablespoons for coating berries

1 tablespoon baking powder

½ teaspoon salt

2 cups blueberries

4 tablespoons (½ stick) unsalted butter, softened

4 tablespoons vegetable shortening

1½ cups sugar

2 large eggs, at room temperature

1 cup milk

¼ teaspoon almond extract

TOPPING

12 tablespoons vegetable shortening

1½ cups sugar

1 cup sifted all-purpose flour

1½ teaspoons cinnamon

Corn Bread

Served warm with butter and jam, you can't fit more down-home comfort in a 9-inch pan.

1½ cups all-purpose flour

1 teaspoon baking soda

4 teaspoons baking powder

3 tablespoons sugar

1½ teaspoons salt

1½ cups yellow cornmeal

½ teaspoon nutmeg

3 large eggs, lightly beaten

1½ cups buttermilk

5 tablespoons vegetable shortening, melted

Preheat oven to 425 degrees.

Lightly grease a 9-inch square baking pan.

In a large bowl, sift together the flour, baking soda, baking powder, sugar, and salt. Add in the cornmeal and nutmeg, mixing to combine. Stir in the eggs, buttermilk, and shortening, thoroughly mixing all ingredients. Batter may be lumpy.

Pour the batter into the prepared pan and bake for 25 to 30 minutes until lightly golden, or until a cake tester inserted into the center of bread comes out with moist crumbs attached. Serve hot.

MAKES 1 BREAD; SERVES 6 TO 8.

Lemon Poppy Seed Quick Bread

Preheat oven to 350 degrees.

Grease and flour a 9 x 5 x 3-inch loaf pan.

In a medium-size bowl, combine the flour, sugar, baking powder, and salt. Set aside.

In a large bowl, mix together the milk, eggs, zest, and butter. Stir in the vanilla and lemon extracts. Add in the dry ingredients and mix well. Add the poppy seeds.

Pour the batter into the prepared pan. Sprinkle the top with the reserved tablespoon of sugar. Bake for about 1 hour, or until a cake tester inserted into the center of loaf comes out clean. Let cool for 20 minutes before serving.

MAKES 1 LOAF; SERVES 8 TO 10.

3 cups all-purpose flour

1 cup sugar plus 1 tablespoon for sprinkling

1 tablespoon baking powder

1 teaspoon salt

1 cup milk

2 large eggs, lightly beaten

2 tablespoons grated lemon zest

6 tablespoons (¾ stick) unsalted butter, melted

½ teaspoon vanilla extract

¼ teaspoon lemon extract

½ cup poppy seeds

Orange Glazed Muffins

A delightful, light-as-a-feather muffin that's equally good with or without the glaze.

MUFFINS

2½ cups all-purpose flour

2 teaspoons baking powder

½ teaspoon baking soda

½ teaspoon salt

8 tablespoons vegetable shortening

1 cup sugar

2 large eggs, at room temperature

1 cup orange juice

2 tablespoons grated orange zest

1 cup finely chopped pecans

GLAZE

1½ cups confectioners' sugar

2 tablespoons water (more if needed)

GARNISH

1 cup coarsely chopped pecans

Preheat oven to 375 degrees.

Generously grease a 12-cup muffin tin.

In a medium bowl, sift together the flour, baking powder, baking soda, and salt. Set aside.

In a large bowl, on the medium speed of an electric mixer, cream the shortening for about 1 minute, gradually adding the sugar. Beat in the eggs. Add the dry ingredients in two parts, alternating with orange juice, mixing after each addition until blended. Stir in the zest and pecans.

Fill the muffin cups about three-quarters full. Bake for 20 to 25 minutes, until lightly golden, or until a cake tester inserted into the center of a muffin comes out with moist crumbs attached. Do not overbake. Allow muffins to cool for about 20 minutes.

To make the glaze, stir together the sugar and water in a small bowl until smooth. Drizzle the glaze over the muffins and sprinkle generously with chopped nuts.

MAKES 12 MUFFINS.

Raspberry Cream Cheese Buns

> *I don't think I've worked a day at Buttercup without having one of these for breakfast—in fact, they're usually eaten by the entire staff, so we always have to bake a double batch just to have some on hand for the customers!*

Preheat oven to 350 degrees.

Grease and flour a *large* (1-cup capacity) 12-cup muffin tin.

In a medium bowl, combine 1 cup of the flour, baking soda, baking powder, and salt. Set aside.

In a large bowl, on the low speed of an electric mixer, beat the cream cheese, butter, and sugar until fluffy, about 2 to 3 minutes. Beat in the eggs, one at a time. Stir in the vanilla. Add in the dry ingredients, alternating with the milk. Add in the additional ¾ cup of flour until well combined.

Spoon the batter into muffin cups. Spoon 3 small dollops of raspberry preserves on top of each bun. Using a small knife, swirl the preserves into the batter to form a marbled effect. Bake for 20 to 25 minutes, or until a cake tester inserted into the center of a bun comes out clean. Do not overbake.

MAKES 12 BUNS.

1 cup all-purpose flour

1 teaspoon baking soda

½ teaspoon baking powder

¼ teaspoon salt

8 ounces (1 package) cream cheese, softened

½ cup (1 stick) unsalted butter, softened

1 cup sugar

2 large eggs, at room temperature

½ teaspoon vanilla extract

¼ cup milk

¾ cup all-purpose flour

¼ to ⅓ cup raspberry preserves

Sour Cream Coffee Cake

You'll be amazed at the texture of this superb coffee cake—perfect for breakfast, dessert, afternoon snack, or anytime.

CAKE

1½ cups sour cream, at room temperature

1½ teaspoons baking soda

3 cups all-purpose flour

1½ teaspoons baking powder

6 tablespoons (¾ stick) unsalted butter, softened

6 tablespoons vegetable shortening

1½ cups sugar

3 large eggs, at room temperature

1½ teaspoons vanilla extract

TOPPING

¾ cup finely chopped walnuts

½ cup sugar

1½ teaspoons cinnamon

Preheat oven to 350 degrees.

Grease and flour a 9 x 13–inch baking pan.

To prepare the cake, combine the sour cream and baking soda. Set aside.

Sift the flour and baking powder in a medium bowl and set aside.

In a large bowl, on the medium speed of an electric mixer, cream the butter and shortening until smooth, about 2 minutes. Gradually add the sugar and continue beating 2 minutes more. Add in the eggs, one at a time. Add dry ingredients to the batter alternately with the sour cream mixture until well combined. Stir in the vanilla.

Pour the batter into the prepared pan. Combine the topping ingredients and sprinkle over the entire top of the cake. Bake 40 to 50 minutes, or until a cake tester inserted into the center of the cake comes out clean. Let cool for 20 minutes before serving.

MAKES 1 CAKE; SERVES 10 TO 12.

Strawberry Banana Muffins

Preheat oven to 375 degrees.

Grease and lightly flour a 12-cup muffin tin.

In a medium bowl, combine the flour, nutmeg, and salt. Set aside.

In a large bowl, on the low speed of an electric mixer, cream the butter and sugar until fluffy, about 3 minutes. Add in the mashed bananas and the baking soda mixture and beat until well incorporated. Add in the dry ingredients and mix until just combined, being careful not to overmix. Batter may be lumpy. Gently fold the strawberries into the batter.

Fill the muffin cups about three-quarters full. Bake for 18 to 22 minutes until lightly golden, or until a cake tester inserted into the center of a muffin comes out with moist crumbs attached. Do not overbake.

MAKES 12 MUFFINS.

2¼ cups all-purpose flour

1½ teaspoons nutmeg

¼ teaspoon salt

¾ cup (1½ sticks) unsalted butter, softened

¾ cup sugar

1½ cups mashed bananas (about 2 small bananas)

1½ teaspoons baking soda dissolved in 1½ tablespoons hot water

1½ cups washed, hulled, and sliced strawberries

Traditional Southern Biscuits

Believe it or not, these are quite simple and quick to make. You'll impress your family or guests when you tell them you've just whipped up a batch of fresh biscuits to go with dinner!

2 cups all-purpose flour
1 tablespoon baking powder
1 teaspoon salt
⅓ cup vegetable shortening
1 cup milk or buttermilk

Preheat oven to 450 degrees.

In a large bowl, sift together the flour, baking powder, and salt. Using a pastry blender or two forks, cut in the shortening. Pour in the milk all at once and stir until just mixed. Add droplets more of milk if dough is dry. Gather the dough into a ball and place on a floured surface. Sprinkle with flour if necessary to make dough less sticky. Roll with a rolling pin to a ½-inch thickness. Using a round biscuit cutter, cut and place biscuits on lightly greased baking sheets.

Bake for 10 to 12 minutes or until golden brown. Serve right away, with plenty of butter.

MAKES 12 BISCUITS.

Whole Wheat Maple Syrup Muffins

Preheat oven to 375 degrees.

Grease a 12-cup muffin tin generously with butter.

In a large bowl, mix together the dry ingredients, making a well in the center. Stir in the liquid ingredients until just combined, being careful not to overmix. Batter may be lumpy.

Fill the muffin cups about three-quarters full. Bake for 14 to 16 minutes, until lightly golden, or until a cake tester inserted into the center of a muffin comes out with moist crumbs attached. Do not overbake.

MAKES 12 MUFFINS.

1½ cups whole wheat flour

¾ cup cake flour

2 teaspoons baking powder

½ teaspoon baking soda

½ teaspoon salt

3 large eggs, lightly beaten

3 tablespoons honey

3 tablespoons maple syrup

¾ cup corn oil or vegetable oil

1 cup plus 2 tablespoons milk

1½ teaspoons vanilla extract

Seasonal Desserts

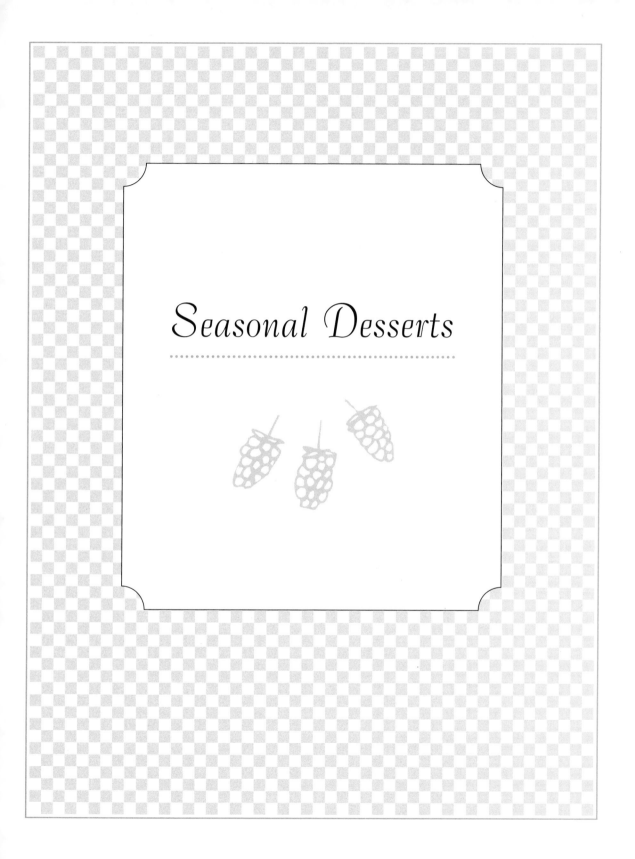

Gingerbread

This recipe was developed after getting numerous customer requests last winter for a good gingerbread loaf—perfect for holiday gatherings.

Preheat oven to 350 degrees.

Grease and lightly flour a 9 x 5 x 3-inch loaf pan.

In a medium bowl, combine the flour, baking soda, salt, and spices. Set aside.

In a large bowl, on the medium speed of an electric mixer, cream the butter and brown sugar until fluffy, about 2 to 3 minutes. Beat in the eggs one at a time. Add the dry ingredients in two parts, alternating with the buttermilk. Stir in the molasses and vanilla.

Pour the batter into the prepared pan and bake 30 to 40 minutes, or until a cake tester inserted into the center of loaf comes out clean. Let cool in pan for 20 minutes. Remove from pan and cool completely on a wire rack.

MAKES 1 LOAF; SERVES 8 TO 10.

1 ½ cups all-purpose flour

½ teaspoon baking soda

¼ teaspoon salt

1 tablespoon ground ginger

2 teaspoons cinnamon

¼ teaspoon allspice

½ cup (1 stick) unsalted butter, softened

½ cup firmly packed light brown sugar

2 large eggs, at room temperature

½ cup buttermilk

1 tablespoon light unsulfured molasses

2 teaspoons vanilla extract

Glazed Pumpkin Squares

These moist, cakey bars are the perfect fall treat. Pumpkin purists can omit the glaze.

CAKE

1¾ cups all-purpose flour

2 teaspoons baking powder

½ teaspoon salt

1 teaspoon cinnamon

¼ teaspoon nutmeg

¼ teaspoon ground ginger

4 tablespoons (½ stick) unsalted butter, softened

¾ cup sugar

2 large eggs, at room temperature

½ cup unsweetened applesauce

¾ cup pumpkin puree (cooked fresh or canned)

1 tablespoon grated orange zest

½ cup golden raisins

GLAZE

1½ cups confectioners' sugar

2 tablespoons water (more if needed)

Preheat oven to 350 degrees.

Grease and flour a 9 x 13-inch baking pan.

In a medium bowl, combine the flour, baking powder, salt, and spices. Set aside.

In a large bowl, on the medium speed of an electric mixer, cream the butter and sugar until fluffy, about 2 to 3 minutes. Add the eggs, one at a time. Beat in the applesauce and the pumpkin puree until well incorporated. Add in the dry ingredients and combine thoroughly. Stir in the zest and raisins.

Pour the batter into the prepared pan and bake for 18 to 22 minutes, or until a cake tester inserted into the center of the pan comes out clean.

To make the glaze, stir together the sugar and water in a small bowl until smooth. Drizzle the glaze over the squares in a decorative fashion. Allow to cool to room temperature before cutting and serving.

MAKES TWELVE 3-INCH SQUARES.

Macaroons

A delicious version of these traditional holiday cookies.

Preheat oven to 300 degrees.

Line two 12 x 18-inch baking sheets with aluminum foil.

Place the almond paste in a food processor and process for about 1 minute. Slowly blend in the sugar and egg whites. Add the confectioners' sugar and flour.

Drop by rounded teaspoonfuls onto the prepared cookie sheets, leaving several inches between for expansion. Bake for 25 to 30 minutes or until lightly golden. Cool cookies on the sheets for 1 minute. Remove to a rack to cool completely.

MAKES ABOUT 5 DOZEN COOKIES.

1 cup almond paste
¾ cup sugar
2 large egg whites
⅓ cup confectioners' sugar
2 tablespoons all-purpose flour

New Year's Honey Cake

Old-fashioned cakes are best loved at holiday time. Here's a wonderful honey cake that's been around in my family for a couple of generations; it can also be made in two loaf pans, making it ideal for a holiday gift.

3½ cups cake flour

1 tablespoon baking powder

½ teaspoon salt

1 tablespoon cinnamon

½ teaspoon ground cloves

¼ teaspoon nutmeg

1 cup vegetable oil

1 cup honey

1½ cups sugar

½ cup firmly packed light brown sugar

3 large eggs, lightly beaten

1 teaspoon vanilla extract

¼ teaspoon almond extract

1 cup brewed strong tea

½ cup orange juice

3 tablespoons brandy

½ cup sliced, blanched almonds

Preheat oven to 350 degrees.

Lightly grease a 10-inch tube pan.

In a large bowl, whisk together the flour, baking powder, salt, and spices. Make a well in the center and add the remaining ingredients, in order, except the almonds. Mix on the low speed of an electric mixer, making sure all of the ingredients are thoroughly incorporated.

Pour the batter into the prepared pan. Sprinkle the top evenly with the almonds. Bake 60 to 70 minutes, or until a cake tester inserted into the center of cake comes out clean. Let cake cool in pan for 20 minutes. Remove from pan and cool completely on a wire rack.

MAKES ONE 10-INCH CAKE; SERVES 12 TO 14.

Plain Ol' Fudge

Lightly grease a 9 x 13-inch baking pan.

Place the chocolate chips, marshmallow cream, vanilla, butter, and walnuts in a large bowl. Mix well. In a heavy-bottomed saucepan, place the evaporated milk and sugar. On a low flame, let the milk mixture boil for about 6 minutes, stirring constantly. Pour this over the chocolate mixture and stir until well blended. Pour into the prepared pan. Refrigerate for 1 hour before cutting and serving.

MAKES ABOUT TWENTY-FOUR 2-INCH SQUARES.

4 cups semisweet chocolate chips

1 (8-ounce) jar marshmallow cream

1 teaspoon vanilla extract

4 tablespoons (½ stick) unsalted butter, softened

2 cups coarsely chopped walnuts

1 (12-ounce) can evaporated milk

4½ cups sugar

Pumpkin Pie

Nothing says Thanksgiving like pumpkin pie. Serve this one with whipped cream or vanilla ice cream if desired.

CRUST

1½ cups all-purpose flour

1 tablespoon sugar

¼ teaspoon salt

½ cup (1 stick) cold unsalted butter, cut into small pieces

2 to 3 tablespoons ice water

FILLING

2 cups pumpkin puree (cooked fresh or canned)

3 large eggs, at room temperature

¼ cup sugar

¾ cup firmly packed light brown sugar

½ teaspoon salt

1½ teaspoons cinnamon

1 teaspoon ground ginger

½ teaspoon nutmeg

¼ teaspoon ground cloves

¼ cup milk

¾ cup evaporated milk

Preheat oven to 400 degrees.

To make the crust: Place the flour, sugar, and salt in a large bowl and, using a pastry blender, cut in the butter until the mixture resembles coarse cornmeal. Sprinkle the ice water by tablespoons over the flour mixture, tossing with a fork until all of the dough is moistened. Form dough into a ball. On a lightly floured surface, roll out the dough to fit into a 9-inch glass pie dish. Fold the edges under all around the rim and crimp.

To make the filling: On the low speed of an electric mixer, beat the pumpkin puree and eggs until smooth. Add the sugars, salt, and spices and blend well. Add the milk and the evaporated milk gradually, beating until smooth.

Pour into the prepared pie shell and bake for 40 to 45 minutes, or until a cake tester inserted into the center of pie comes out clean. Remove from oven and let pie cool on a rack for at least 30 minutes. Serve slightly warm.

MAKES ONE 9-INCH PIE; SERVES 6 TO 8.

Red Velvet Cake

*"A yellow cake with a hint of cocoa, dyed a deep beautiful red,"
is the answer to the most frequently asked question at Buttercup.
Some of you may know Red Velvet as the Armadillo Cake from
the movie Steel Magnolias; others may know it as the
best cake they've ever tasted!*

Preheat oven to 350 degrees.

Grease and lightly flour three 9 x 2-inch round cake pans, then line the bottoms with waxed paper.

In a small bowl, whisk together until well combined the food coloring, cocoa powder, and vanilla. Set aside.

In a large bowl, on the medium speed of an electric mixer, cream the butter and sugar until very fluffy, about 4 to 5 minutes. Add in the eggs, one at a time. Add the flour in three parts, alternating with the buttermilk, beating well after each addition. Add in the salt. Beat in the cocoa mixture until thoroughly incorporated.

In a small bowl, mix together the vinegar and baking soda. Add to the batter at the end, making sure to mix well.

Divide the batter among the prepared pans. Bake for 20 to 25 minutes, or until a cake tester inserted into the center of the cake comes out clean. Let cake cool in pans for 10 minutes. Remove from pans and cool completely on wire rack.

When cake has cooled, ice between the layers, then ice top and sides of cake with Red Velvet Icing.

MAKES 1 THREE-LAYER 9-INCH CAKE; SERVES 10 TO 12.

¼ cup red food coloring

2 tablespoons unsweetened cocoa powder

1 teaspoon vanilla extract

½ cup (1 stick) unsalted butter, softened

1½ cups sugar

2 large eggs, at room temperature

2¼ cups cake flour

1 cup buttermilk

1 teaspoon salt

1 teaspoon apple cider vinegar

1 teaspoon baking soda

Red Velvet Icing (page 118)

Snickerdoodles

What would Christmas be without these delectable favorites?

2¾ cups all-purpose flour

2 teaspoons cream of tartar

1 teaspoon baking soda

¼ teaspoon salt

1 cup vegetable shortening

1½ cups sugar plus 1
  tablespoon for sprinkling

2 large eggs, at room
  temperature

¼ teaspoon vanilla extract

1 tablespoon cinnamon

Preheat oven to 350 degrees.

In a medium bowl, sift together the flour, cream of tartar, baking soda, and salt. Set aside.

In a large bowl, cream the shortening with the sugar until fluffy, about 2 to 3 minutes. Add the eggs one at a time and mix well. Add the vanilla. Add in the flour mixture and beat thoroughly. Refrigerate the dough for 1 hour. Roll the dough into balls about 1 inch in diameter. Roll the balls in a combination of the remaining sugar and the cinnamon.

Place on ungreased cookie sheets, leaving several inches between for expansion. Bake for 10 to 12 minutes or until lightly golden. Cool cookies on the sheets for 1 minute, then remove to a rack to cool completely.

MAKES ABOUT 4 TO 5 DOZEN COOKIES.

White Fudge with Walnuts and Dried Cranberries

This is a great holiday treat to give as a gift, or to nibble on while wrapping presents.

Lightly grease an 8 x 8-inch baking pan.

In a medium saucepan over low heat, melt the chips with the butter.

On the medium speed of an electric mixer, cream the sugar, the cream cheese, and the buttercream until smooth, about 2 minutes. Blend in the melted chips. Stir in the remaining ingredients.

Pour into the prepared pan. Refrigerate for 1 hour (or more) before cutting and serving.

MAKES ABOUT SIXTEEN 2-INCH SQUARES.

4 cups vanilla chips or white chocolate chips

4 tablespoons (½ stick) unsalted butter

1 cup sifted confectioners' sugar

6 ounces cream cheese, softened

1 cup vanilla buttercream (store-bought, or make your own)

1½ cups chopped walnuts

1½ cups dried cranberries

1 tablespoon orange zest

Puddings
and
Custards

Banana Pudding with Nilla Wafers

Well, folks, here it is—you begged, you pleaded, some of you even shed tears! How much can a person take? This phenomenal recipe has been around for generations, and has been making people weak at the knees with its delectable flavor and texture. Make sure to prepare it in the morning for later that day, because the pudding has to set.

On the low speed of an electric mixer, blend the water, milk, and pudding powder until thoroughly mixed, about 1 minute. Refrigerate for at least 4 hours (or overnight) until firm.

In a separate bowl, whip the heavy cream until soft peaks form. Gently fold the pudding mixture into the whipped cream until well incorporated.

In a large bowl, starting with the wafers, make five to six layers with Nilla wafers, sliced bananas, and then the pudding mixture, until all of the pudding mixture is gone. End with pudding and decorate with crushed wafers on top if desired. Refrigerate about 30 minutes before serving, and refrigerate any leftovers.

SERVES 10 TO 12.

1½ cups cold water

1 (14-ounce) can sweetened condensed milk

⅔ cup instant vanilla pudding powder

3 cups heavy cream

One box Nilla wafers

3 to 4 medium bananas, sliced

Cherry Pudding

A twist on bread pudding, cherries make this a lovely cool summer-evening dessert.

2 cups coarse bread crumbs
(coarsely cut day-old
white bread will do)

4 cups milk

3 tablespoons unsalted butter,
cut into small pieces

4 large eggs, lightly beaten

1½ cups sugar

4 cups fresh sweet cherries,
pitted

Preheat oven to 350 degrees.

Lightly grease a 2-quart baking dish. Place the bread crumbs inside.

In a medium saucepan, heat the milk until scalded (a crinkly film forms on top). Pour this over the bread crumbs. Toss in the remaining ingredients and stir gently to combine.

Bake for 45 to 50 minutes, or until well set and golden.

SERVES 6 TO 8.

Chocolate Pudding

To me, there's no dessert more deserving of the title "comfort food" than chocolate pudding. I like mine warm, practically straight out of the pot, although you can refrigerate it and serve it cold, especially with a little whipped cream if you like.

In a heavy-bottomed saucepan, mix together the sugar, cocoa powder, cornstarch, and salt. Add half of the milk and whisk over medium heat until the mixture is smooth. Add the remaining milk and continue whisking over medium heat until pudding thickens and comes to a boil, about 10 minutes. Stir continuously for about 1 minute on a low boil.

Remove from heat and add the chocolate and the vanilla, stirring until chocolate melts completely. Refrigerate uncovered for at least 2 hours until chilled.

SERVES 4 TO 6.

1⅓ cups sugar

½ cup unsweetened cocoa powder

⅓ cup cornstarch

⅛ teaspoon salt

4 cups milk

1 ounce semisweet chocolate, finely chopped

1 tablespoon plus 1 teaspoon vanilla extract

Coconut Pudding

An unusual pudding, in my opinion,
chock-full of textures and flavor.

1 cup coarse bread crumbs
(coarsely cut day-old
white bread will do)

1 cup sweetened, shredded
coconut

4 cups hot (not scalded) milk

2 tablespoons unsalted butter,
melted

2 large eggs, lightly beaten

¼ cup plus 2 tablespoons
sugar

1 teaspoon cornstarch

Grated zest of ½ lemon

Preheat oven to 375 degrees.

Lightly grease a 2-quart baking dish.

Soak the bread crumbs and the coconut in the hot milk for 1 hour. Toss in the remaining ingredients and stir gently to combine.

Pour into the prepared dish and bake for 45 to 50 minutes, or until well set and golden.

SERVES 6 TO 8.

Old-Fashioned Bread Pudding

For a more custardy version of this classic, use 4 cups of milk and 2 cups of bread crumbs; the baking time increases about 10 minutes or so.

Preheat oven to 350 degrees.

Lightly grease a 2-quart baking dish. Place the bread crumbs inside.

In a heavy-bottomed saucepan, place the milk and the vanilla. Allow to simmer on medium heat until scalded (a crinkly film forms on top). Pour this over the bread crumbs and stir. Allow to cool for about 10 minutes. Add the remaining ingredients and stir to combine.

Bake 40 to 45 minutes, or until cake tester inserted into the center of pudding comes out clean.

SERVES 6 TO 8.

3 cups coarse bread crumbs (coarsely cut day-old white bread will do)

3 cups milk

½ teaspoon vanilla extract

4 tablespoons (½ stick) unsalted butter, melted

½ cup sugar

2 large eggs, lightly beaten

¼ teaspoon salt

1 cup golden raisins

1 teaspoon cinnamon

Rice Pudding

While a bit of labor goes into this dish, you'll consider it a labor of love once you've tasted my favorite recipe for rice pudding.

2 large eggs, at room temperature

½ cup sugar

¼ teaspoon salt

2 cups milk

½ teaspoon cinnamon

½ teaspoon nutmeg, plus additional for sprinkling

1 teaspoon vanilla extract

2 cups cooked rice, on the mushy side (short-grain white or basmati)

½ cup heavy cream

Preheat oven to 350 degrees.

Lightly grease a 2-quart baking dish.

In a medium bowl, lightly beat the eggs, sugar, and salt. Set aside.

In a heavy-bottomed saucepan, place the milk, cinnamon, nutmeg, and vanilla. Allow to simmer on medium heat until scalded (a crinkly film forms on top). Pour this into the egg mixture and stir. Then mix in the rice.

Pour into the prepared dish and set in a baking pan with 1 inch of water. Sprinkle a little nutmeg over the top. Bake 35 to 45 minutes, stirring every 15 minutes or so. Remove from oven and allow to set for about 20 minutes.

Meanwhile, whip the heavy cream on the low speed of an electric mixer until soft peaks form. After the pudding has cooled, stir in the whipped cream. Sprinkle with a little more nutmeg if desired.

SERVES 6 TO 8.

Soft Vanilla Custard

You'll devour this custard as is, or use it as a filling for layer cakes, or to adorn something simple, like a cookie.

In a medium bowl, combine the sugar, flour, and salt. Set aside.

In a heavy-bottomed saucepan, place the milk and allow to simmer on medium heat until scalded (a crinkly film forms on top). Gradually add the milk into the dry ingredients, stirring constantly, and blend well. Pour mixture back into the saucepan and cook over low heat, stirring constantly, for about 5 minutes.

Add a little of the hot mixture into the egg yolks and stir briskly. Pour the yolk mixture back into the saucepan and cook for 2 minutes more, stirring constantly, until thickened. Remove from heat, and add the vanilla and the butter. Cool completely before using.

SERVES 4 TO 6.

½ cup sugar

3 tablespoons all-purpose flour

⅛ teaspoon salt

1 cup milk

2 egg yolks, lightly beaten

2 teaspoons vanilla extract

2 tablespoons unsalted butter

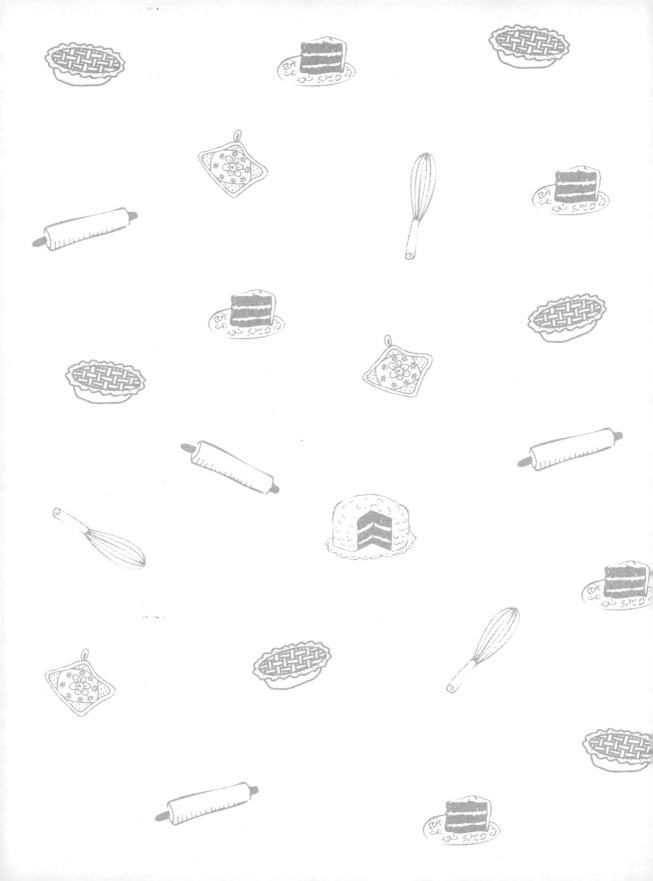

Fillings and Frostings

This simple glaze is ideal for Angel Food Cake (page 21) or any other unadorned dessert.

Bittersweet Chocolate Glaze

In a medium saucepan over low heat, melt the chocolate and the butter (or cream) together, stirring occasionally until completely melted. Remove from heat and stir in desired liquor. Use immediately over completely cooled dessert. Allow to set for 15 minutes. Can be refrigerated and reheated gently if necessary.

4 ounces bittersweet chocolate

4 tablespoons (½ stick) butter or heavy cream

1 to 2 tablespoons brandy, rum, or any liquor of choice

Caramel

1 cup cold water
3 cups sugar
2 cups heavy cream

Combine the water and sugar in a medium saucepan. Set over medium-low heat, stirring occasionally, until the sugar dissolves (about 3 minutes), making sure no sugar is sticking to the sides of the pan. Increase heat to high and boil without stirring, until the syrup becomes a deep amber color, about 15 minutes. To prevent the syrup from becoming grainy, use a pastry brush dipped into cold water to brush down any sugar crystals sticking to the sides of the pan. Swirl the pan occasionally for even browning.

Once the syrup turns deep amber in color, immediately remove from heat. Slowly and carefully add the cream to the syrup (mixture will bubble vigorously), whisking constantly, until cream is incorporated.

Return the pan to medium-low heat, stirring until sauce is smooth, about 1 minute.

Remove from heat and allow to come to room temperature before refrigerating. Can be stored for up to 1 month in refrigerator.

MAKES 3½ CUPS.

Chocolate Whipped Cream Frosting

It's best to use cream that is very cold for whipping. While this icing can be refrigerated, it's better if used the same day.

In a mixing bowl, combine the cream and vanilla. In another bowl, sift the sugar and cocoa together. Then add them to the cream and vanilla. On the medium speed of an electric mixer, whip until soft peaks form but the mixture is stiff enough to spread.

THIS YIELDS ICING FOR 1 TWO- OR THREE-LAYER 9-INCH CAKE.

2 cups heavy cream, chilled
2 teaspoons vanilla extract
¼ cup confectioners' sugar
¼ cup unsweetened cocoa powder

Classic American Buttercream

This sweet vanilla buttercream is ideal for yellow and chocolate cakes or cupcakes.

1 cup (2 sticks) unsalted
  butter, very soft
8 cups confectioners' sugar
½ cup milk
2 teaspoons vanilla extract

Place the butter in a large mixing bowl. Add 4 cups of the sugar and then the milk and vanilla. Beat until smooth and creamy. Gradually add the remaining sugar, 1 cup at a time, until icing is thick enough to be of good spreading consistency (you may not need all of the sugar). If desired, add a few drops of food coloring, and mix thoroughly.

Use and store icing at room temperature, as icing will set if chilled. Can store in an airtight container up to 3 days.

THIS YIELDS ICING FOR 1 TWO- OR THREE-LAYER 9-INCH CAKE,
OR 2 DOZEN CUPCAKES.

Classic Chocolate Buttercream

Beat the butter until creamy, about 3 minutes. Add the milk slowly and beat until smooth. Add the melted chocolate and beat well. Add the vanilla and beat for 3 minutes. Gradually add the sugar and beat until creamy and of desired consistency.

THIS YIELDS ICING FOR 1 TWO- OR THREE-LAYER 9-INCH CAKE, OR 2 DOZEN CUPCAKES.

1 cup (2 sticks) unsalted butter, very soft

1 tablespoon plus 1 teaspoon milk

6 ounces semisweet chocolate, melted and cooled to lukewarm

1 teaspoon vanilla extract

1¼ cups sifted confectioners' sugar

Cream Cheese Icing

A classic that goes with Carrot Cake (page 27), Applesauce Layer Cake (page 23), Sour Cream Spice Cake (page 35), or any other spicy cake recipe.

1 pound (2 8-ounce packages) cream cheese, softened slightly, cut into small pieces

½ cup (1 stick) unsalted butter, softened slightly, cut into small pieces

1½ teaspoons vanilla extract

5 cups sifted confectioners' sugar

In a medium bowl, on the medium speed of an electric mixer, beat the cream cheese and butter until smooth, about 3 minutes. Add the vanilla extract. Gradually add the sugar and beat until well incorporated.

THIS YIELDS ICING FOR 1 TWO- OR THREE-LAYER 9-INCH CAKE.

Honey Glaze

I like this over Angel Food Cake (page 21), Aunt Sadie's Fabulous Pound Cake (page 24), or New Year's Honey Cake (page 88).

Over a low flame, warm the honey in a small saucepan until runny (about 1 minute). Then stir in the sugar and lemon juice. Pour immediately over desired dessert.

2 tablespoons honey
½ cup sifted confectioners' sugar
1 tablespoon lemon juice

Lemon Cream Cheese Icing

Toasting the coconut for about 5 to 8 minutes in the oven really enhances the flavor of this icing.

2 pounds (4 8-ounce packages) cream cheese, softened slightly, cut into small pieces

½ cup (1 stick) unsalted butter, softened slightly, cut into small pieces

1 tablespoon lemon juice

2 teaspoons lemon zest

2 cups sweetened, shredded coconut, toasted

4 to 5 cups sifted confectioners' sugar

In a medium bowl, on the medium speed of an electric mixer, beat the cream cheese and butter until smooth, about 3 minutes. Add the lemon juice and zest. Gradually add the coconut and sugar and beat until well incorporated.

THIS YIELDS ICING FOR 1 TWO- OR THREE-LAYER 9-INCH CAKE.

Milk Chocolate Icing

This light chocolaty icing will complement a wide variety of cakes.

In a small saucepan, combine the butter with the milk chocolate and stir over low heat, until melted and completely smooth. Stir in the cocoa powder and mix thoroughly. Remove from heat and allow to cool for 10 minutes or so.

Pour the chocolate mixture into a large bowl with half the sugar and half the milk. Beat on the medium speed of an electric mixture until smooth.

Add the remaining sugar and milk, as well as the vanilla, and continue beating until smooth. Add extra sugar if needed and beat until creamy and of desired consistency.

THIS YIELDS ICING FOR 1 TWO- OR THREE-LAYER 9-INCH CAKE.

¾ cup (1½ sticks) unsalted butter

6 ounces milk chocolate

1 cup unsweetened cocoa powder

6 to 7 cups (or more) sifted confectioners' sugar

1 cup hot scalded milk

2 teaspoons vanilla extract

Orange Curd Filling

Lovely on its own, this curd is also nice as an accompaniment to my Fireside Orange Cake (page 28) or Angel Food Cake (page 21).

10 large egg yolks, at room temperature

2 large whole eggs, at room temperature

3 tablespoons grated orange zest

1¼ cups orange juice

¼ teaspoon orange extract

1½ cups sugar

1 cup (2 sticks) unsalted butter, cut into small pieces

Place the first six ingredients in a heavy-bottomed saucepan and whisk to combine thoroughly. Using a wooden spoon, stir constantly over medium heat. Cook about 15 to 20 minutes until thick and bubbly. Remove from heat and add the butter, one piece at a time, stirring to incorporate.

Place in refrigerator until firm and chilled, at least 6 hours (usually overnight).

THIS YIELDS FILLING FOR 1 TWO- OR THREE-LAYER 9-INCH CAKE, ABOUT 5½ CUPS.

Peanut Butter Icing

This icing is great for kids (of any age!).

In a medium bowl, sift together the cocoa powder and sugar. Set aside.

In a large bowl, on the medium speed of an electric mixer, beat the peanut butter, butter, and vanilla until fluffy, about 1 to 2 minutes. Add in the dry ingredients and mix thoroughly, along with the milk. Add droplets more of milk if needed to make the icing smooth.

THIS YIELDS ICING FOR 1 TWO- OR THREE-LAYER 9-INCH CAKE OR 24 CUPCAKES.

10 tablespoons unsweetened cocoa powder

6 cups confectioners' sugar

1½ cups creamy peanut butter

½ cup (1 stick) unsalted butter, softened

1 tablespoon vanilla extract

1 cup plus 1 tablespoon milk, more if necessary

Red Velvet Icing

Buttercup staffers describe this icing as somewhere between buttercream and whipped cream. Long beating makes it light and fluffy, and its not-too-sweet flavor makes it a perfect mate for Red Velvet Cake (page 91) or Milk Chocolate Layer Cake (page 31).

2 cups milk

⅜ cup all-purpose flour

2 cups (4 sticks) unsalted butter, cold

2 cups sugar

2 teaspoons vanilla extract

In a heavy-bottomed saucepan, whisk to combine the milk and flour. Stir constantly over medium-high heat until smooth and thick (anywhere from 12 to 18 minutes). Let the mixture cool for at least 30 minutes. When cool, remove the "skin" that has formed at the top and discard.

While mixture is cooling, on the medium-high speed of an electric mixer, beat the butter and sugar until quite fluffy, about 4 to 5 minutes. Add in the vanilla extract and mix thoroughly. Incorporate the cooled milk mixture in thirds, beating well after each addition.

THIS YIELDS ICING FOR 1 TWO- OR THREE-LAYER 9-INCH CAKE.

Silky Vanilla Buttercream

Also called *Swiss Buttercream*, I've included this recipe for those of you ready for the challenge of a more complicated icing. A candy thermometer is needed for this smooth-as-silk buttercream, which is very elegant and appropriate for special occasions. I use it exclusively for my wedding cakes. I've cut the recipe by two-thirds, which should yield enough for a standard 9-inch cake. Double or triple the ingredients if you're going to tackle a larger confection (and double the time for most components of the recipe).

In a heavy-bottomed saucepan, place the sugar and the water. Cook on medium-high heat until the mixture bubbles and reaches 238 degrees on a candy thermometer (softball stage).

Place the egg whites in a standing mixer bowl and beat on medium speed with the whisk attachment until about double in volume. Turn speed to high and pour in the sugar mixture in a thin, steady stream. Beat for about 10 to 12 minutes or until the bowl has cooled to luke-warm. Reduce mixer speed to low, and add the butter in pieces, making sure each piece is thoroughly incorporated. Beat for another 3 to 4 minutes. Add the vanilla and beat for another minute or so. The mixture should begin to thicken. If not, refrigerate for 10 minutes, then beat again for another 2 minutes.

1 cup sugar
¼ cup cold water
4 large egg whites
2 cups (4 sticks) unsalted butter, cold
2 tablespoons vanilla extract

THIS YIELDS ICING FOR 1 TWO- OR THREE-LAYER 9-INCH CAKE.

White Chocolate Frosting

This easy-to-make frosting will provide a pleasant surprise to those expecting a vanilla buttercream. It goes nicely with white or yellow cake, or especially with White Chocolate Layer Cake (page 36).

½ cup (1 stick) unsalted butter

1¼ cups sugar

1½ cups evaporated milk

2 teaspoons vanilla extract

1 teaspoon cornstarch

4 cups coarsely chopped white chocolate

In a heavy-bottomed saucepan, melt the butter over low heat. When melted, add the sugar and milk and stir thoroughly. Allow the mixture to boil on low heat for 1 minute. Remove from heat and add the vanilla and cornstarch. Pour in the white chocolate, stirring until completely smooth. Allow to cool for about 30 minutes, and then refrigerate for about 1 hour. Beat gently with a hand mixer to make the icing smooth if necessary.

THIS YIELDS ICING FOR 1 TWO- OR THREE-LAYER 9-INCH CAKE.

INDEX

INDEX

custard, soft vanilla, 103

* * *

dates, applesauce cookies with raisins and, 41

* * *

filling:
  for apple butter apple pie, 57
  for apple cobbler, 58
  for butterscotch pie, 59
  cream cheese, for cream cheese swirl brownies, 44
  for fresh peach pie, 61
  for German chocolate pie, 62
  for Lady Baltimore cake, 29–30
  for lemon meringue pie, 63
  for Mom's summer icebox pie, 64
  for old-fashioned buttermilk pie, 65
  orange curd, 116
  for peanut butter chocolate mud pie, 60
  for pumpkin pie, 90
  for strawberry rhubarb pie, 67
  for two-crust cherry pie, 68
fireside orange cake with brandy glaze, 28
fresh peach pie, 61

frosting:
  brown sugar, caramel cake with, 26
  chocolate whipped cream, 109
  for Lady Baltimore cake, 29–30
  white chocolate, 120
  see also buttercream; glaze; icing
fudge:
  plain ol', 89
  white, with walnuts and dried cranberries, 93

* * *

German chocolate pie, 62
gingerbread, 85
gingersnaps, 45
glaze:
  for apple pecan cake, 22
  bittersweet chocolate, 107
  brandy, fireside orange cake with, 28
  for glazed pumpkin squares, 86
  honey, 113
  for orange glazed muffins, 76
  see also buttercream; frosting; icing
glazed:
  muffins, orange, 76
  pumpkin squares, 86
golden layer cake, Buttercup, 25

greatest brownies ever, 53

* * *

Heath bar peanut butter pecan cookies, 50
hermits, 46
honey:
  cake, New Year's, 88
  glaze, 113

* * *

icebox pie, Mom's summer, 64
icing:
  cream cheese, 112
  hints for, 18
  lemon cream cheese, 114
  milk chocolate, 115
  peanut butter, 117
  red velvet, 118
  see also buttercream; frosting; glaze

* * *

Lady Baltimore cake, 29–30
layer cake:
  applesauce, 23
  Buttercup golden, 25
  hints for, 16–17
  milk chocolate, 31
  "over the top" chocolate, 33
  white, with chocolate chips, 37
  white chocolate, 36
lemon:
  cream cheese icing, 114
  meringue bars, 47